SECRET PORTLAND, OREGON

A Guide to the Weird, Wonderful, and Obscure

Jeff Brawn

Reedy Press
PO Box 5131
St. Louis, MO 63139
www.reedypress.com

Library of Congress Control Number: 2022937103
ISBN: 9781681064055

Design by Jill Halpin
Unless otherwise noted, all images are courtesy of the author or blieved to be in the public domain.

Printed in the United States of America
22 23 24 25 26   5 4 3 2 1

This book is dedicated to three brave women who risked the Oregon Trail with me to become Portland settlers: my wife, Jeanne, and our daughters, Riley and Quinn. They let me borrow against their courage as I had none of my own. And to my late aunt, Lucinda Brawn, who left me two pack mules and a covered wagon in her will.

CONTENTS

ACKNOWLEDGMENTS

Any acknowledgment section for a book like this would be incomplete without acknowledging that everything mentioned within has occurred on the stolen land of its indigenous peoples. The Multnomah, Kathlamet, Clackamas, Cowlitz of Chinook, Tualatin Kalapuya, Molalla, and certainly other tribes made their home here along our rivers. Portland has one of the largest Urban Native American populations with over 380 tribes represented in our metropolitan area.

I couldn't have written this book without the kind and helpful natures that I find in nearly all Portlanders. Well, I *could* have, but it would have been so much less rich. I don't know most of their names. They were bagging my groceries or standing near me at a scenic overlook or waving a metal detector over my luggage at the airport. I ask a lot of questions everywhere I go, and Portlanders have been wonderful at providing answers.

A few names of people I do know to thank:

- Wetland warrior Mike Houck for his dedication to saving our urban green spaces and donating material to this book.
- Jason de Parrie-Turner, president of Weird Portland United (because there is such a thing), who was invaluable.
- Jason DeSomer, a gifted Portland photographer who shared some amazing photos with us (www.whatever.photo).
- I couldn't have gotten the photos needed during the pandemic without the help of photographers Jason Moore (commons.wikimedia.org/wiki/User:Another_Believer) and Ian Sane (iansane.smugmug.com).
- Erik Gauger for sharing his research and stunning photos. His travel blog, notesfromtheroad.com is a site you'll want to visit.
- Sara Sjol and Tiffany Conklin at Portland Street Alliance.
- Olivier Bouwman for being so helpful.
- Jim Stewart, curator of the Zymoglyphic Museum, for being the real deal and sharing his collection and insight.

- The amazing people who contribute to the Facebook group Hidden Portland.
- Educator-journalist Finn J. D. John and his work of love and collective good—Offbeat Oregon History (offbeatoregon.com). Go to his website. You will spend days there.

To those I've forgotten, I'll buy you a cider at Reverend Nat's.

INTRODUCTION

Portlanders don't keep anything secret on purpose, except maybe their favorite brunch spot. Portland has the kindest population of any city (maybe tied with Madison, WI). But if you want to get to know the sublayer of the city, unusual or off-trail treasures, you have to do some digging. Why? My theory is that in Portland, most of the things worth seeing are born of passion, creativity, or happenstance—not profit. In other cities, everything within these pages would be monetized, cleaned up, and advertised. Despite the juggernaut of gentrification, Portland is still a city of individualists and idealists. Any "weirdness" is almost always a case of someone being or doing something authentically themselves, and people can sniff out money grabs. Some of the people in this book will flat-out refuse your money. Some ask only for donations.

To be clear, this is my personal perspective, constrained as it needs to be to conform to Reedy Press's *Secret City* series. Left on my own, this book would be 1,000 pages long, never completed, and left unpublished. I initially balked when a friend of mine, an art buyer from the publishing house, asked me to tackle the project, because I didn't grow up here. As I always say, "You don't ask a fish to describe life in the lake, and you don't ask a squirrel. You have to go to a duck if you want perspective." So, this book is my duck's-eye view. Having grown up in the Midwest, I appreciate some things that are invisible or taken for granted by those born locally. Yet having lived here for a number of years now, I have asked enough questions and explored enough to . . . er, write a book. Hopefully the result is a book that has something for the tourist, those born here, and other ducks like myself.

MONDO CROQUET

Want to play croquet, but it feels too snooty and British?

Croquet was first played in Britain with boxwood balls and went by the name Pall Mall. In Portland, we know that Pall Malls are cigarettes and you play croquet with bowling balls. How do you hit the bowling balls without breaking your little mallet? Obviously, you don't use a traditional mallet. You use a sledgehammer. How do those bowling balls go through the tiny wickets? Wickets are not tiny, but made by bending a piece of steel rebar around a telephone pole. It's all very sensible.

Portland's version is known as Mondo Croquet. It was invented by local geniuses Stephen Peter and Mike Shkolnik in the mid '90s. Then in July of 1997, the first annual world championship was held in the North Park Blocks.

Peters and the gang are part of the Cacophony Society, which is something like the Church of the Subgenius from the '80s in that it is an organization that is just slightly organized and seems to exist for the purpose of expanding minds and having fun. It's performance art of a type, built on "pranks, hoaxes, and culture jamming." Santacon is their doing. If you've seen hundreds of Santas mobbing shops, bars, and elevators to delight and/or frighten and annoy citizens, that was them.

Mondo Croquet is the most established thing about this antiestablishment group. Members of the Cacophony Society play regularly throughout the year and host the World Championship of Mondo Croquet. They state that it is always

---

The ultimate goal of the World Mondo Croquet Federation is to get the chance to play at the Summer Olympics.

Mondo Croquet illustration by Jeff Brawn

THE WORLD MONDO CROQUET FEDERATION

What: Portland croquet league, Portland style

Where: North Park Blocks

Cost: The cost of a bowling ball and a sledgehammer to play. Watching is free.

Pro Tip: Visit bowling alleys and see if they'll give you a badly drilled ball for free. Or brave the Goodwill pound store for a previously loved ball.

in Portland and always on the last Sunday in July (although the last one was in August, which is just so . . . Mondo.) The rules are pretty similar to boring croquet except for the equipment. Oh, and the costumes. They prefer to play in costumes. Of course, the equipment leads to a difference in play. You think those sledgehammers would crack those bowling balls? Yep. A lot. So the rules state that you must continue to play with the largest hunk of broken bowling ball remaining. Or, players can choose to allow you another ball if you buy them all a round of drinks.

See? Americans are civilized too.

WELL, I'LL BE HORSE-TIED

What are those metal rings I see occasionally along the sidewalk or on the street, and why is there a plastic pig tied to one of them?

These are artifacts left over from the horsey times. Back in the day, it was much easier to find a parking space in the city, and you didn't even have to pay to tie up your horse to one of the many metal rings around town. These iron (sometimes brass) rings were common on curbs in the 1800s and into the 20th century. Most cities removed them when citizens quit driving their horse-drawn buggies to town. The early to mid-20th century was a time when most people were promoting "progress" and looking toward the future.

But Portland never has been like other towns. Portlanders liked their horsey rings, and when they noticed them disappearing, they popped their corks and did something about it. Today, a city ordinance states that if you put in a new sidewalk or make a repair, you either have to go around those metal rings or replace them right back where you found them. If that's not possible, you have to put that horsey ring as close as is "practical" to its original location.

But Portlanders did not stop there! Preserving the rings was not enough. Some visionaries understood that we need to celebrate them as well. In the fall of 2005, a man named Scott Wayne Indiana (perfect name) was credited with tying

---

The Horse Project was the subject of a 2011 short documentary called *It's a Ring Thing*, which you can view online.

Courtesy of Jason Moore

the first plastic toy horse to a horsey ring in the Pearl District. He said, "I loved the rings and felt that people just weren't noticing them. This was an attempt to shake people out of their routines and get them to notice their surroundings." Scott was correct, of course, and the city of Portland got behind the guerrilla street art movement, quickly deemed the Horse Project. Not only toy horses began appearing, but sometimes bails of hay and other treats for the horses. And why single out horses? Plastic tigers, pigs, hippos (you know all the plastic animals out there, so I'll quit listing them) started popping up, tied to the rings. I've also seen dolls, which is a little macabre but always makes me chuckle.

HORSEY RINGS

What: Beloved public relics

Where: All over town

Cost: Free

Pro Tip: If you're riding an actual horse, you can use these rings for their intended purpose, but you still have to pay the parking meter.

HIPPO HARDWARE

Don't you just love a junk shop where they don't sell any . . . junk?

Hippo Hardware wants to defy definition, but it's primarily a building salvage store. They specialize in architecture, lighting, plumbing, and hardware from 1860 to 1960. But they also sell "collectibles, trinkets, whatnots, and whoziwhatsits depending on what we get in." There are three floors of hardware and whoziwhatsits. I've measured it, and the joint is 30,000 square feet. That's a lot of salvage, sister! And if you're looking for something they don't have, go ahead and ask them. It might be around somewhere or they might be able to find it for you.

As for their history, I can't do better than their website here, so I'll just steal it: "Hippo Hardware was officially established in 1976 after the founders Steven Miller and Stephen Oppenheim decided to turn a life of swashbuckling adventures into a second life of swashbuckling adventures. We live in the local, even for our customers far away. That means you will probably hear a story about burying a Porsche in a state park while you are asking

HIPPO HARDWARE

What: Salvage heaven

Where: 1040 E Burnside St.

Cost: Free to look!

Pro Tip: You can also try trading with them. If they like your treasure you can get cash or store credit. Go for the credit; you will get more bang for your Hippo bucks.

Their junk has been seen in everything from *Northern Exposure* and *Grimm* to *Jackass* and *There Will Be Blood.*

Locals drop in all the time to see the new inventory.

about a faucet, or see photos of our cashier's Saint Bernards while you're paying for a light fixture. We strongly support community projects, teachers, artists, adventurers, dreamers, and one-man bands."

You know what else is cool about Hippo Hardware? They work with film and television professionals as advisors and providers of year-appropriate period pieces.

LOST NIHONMACHI (JAPANTOWN)

Why is the area in Old Town Portland sometimes referred to as Chinatown and other times Japantown?

The area was, in fact, a neighborhood made mostly of Chinese immigrants who settled there in the 1800s. But (and see if this doesn't sound horribly familiar) resentment among whites grew because Chinese immigrants were willing to work cheaper and harder and were therefore taking "their" jobs. So get this—the US government passed the Chinese Exclusion Act, the very first federal legislation to suspend immigration for one particular nationality.

Japanese obviously suffered discrimination as well, but they weren't part of this legislation, so many Japanese moved into the area to fill the new labor gap. At this point, Chinatown became Japantown (or Nihonmachi to those who lived there). Despite discrimination, Japanese families and business owners eventually flourished. By the 1930s, Japanese families were successful proprietors of all kinds of businesses: restaurants, hotels, doctors' offices, and bank services. Living their lives mostly within the confines of Japantown, the residents were shielded to a great degree from the racism that was exploding up and down the West Coast.

The attack on Pearl Harbor changed everything. The FBI showed up within days to arrest people on their "list," and a curfew was imposed on all Japanese, forcing them to stay inside

THE NEW CHINATOWN/ JAPANTOWN

What: Historic district

Where: Old Town

Cost: Free

Pro Tip: The cherry blossoms at the Japanese American Historical Plaza typically bloom in March and April, but that can be off by a few weeks depending on the whims of Portland weather.

Above: *Turn-of-the-century Old Town*
Left: *Gate to Old Chinatown/Japantown*
Courtesy of Daderot

their homes from 8 p.m. to 6 a.m., which killed trade for Japanese-run restaurants, early morning fruit vendors, and most other Japanese businesses. Then came the Japanese concentration camps in February of 1942. All Japanese immigrants and their children were rounded up, forced to forfeit their possessions, and take only what they could carry to their new "homes" with the barbed-wire fences.

During this time, Chinese families repopulated Japantown, so it became Chinatown once again. When the Japanese families were finally released from the camps, they were given $25 and a train ticket home, which was not enough to start over and, besides, many of their homes and businesses were now occupied. Most of the previous residents of Japantown scattered to various parts of Portland or elsewhere. These days, both Chinese and Japanese culture are acknowledged as a vital part of Portland's history. In order to appreciate just some of the contributions of these immigrants, visit the Lan Su Chinese Garden, the Portland Japanese Garden, and the Japanese American Museum at Naito Center in Old Town, or enjoy the cherry blossoms in bloom at the Japanese American Historical Plaza, a stunning memorial to the 12,000 Japanese wrongly imprisoned during World War II.

Between 1942 and 1945, a total of 10 internment camps were opened, holding approximately 120,000 Japanese Americans for varying periods of time.

ZELDA THE BULLDOG

Where do pampered pups like to stay when they're in Portland?

You've probably seen Zelda whether you realize it or not. She graces the face of greeting cards across the nation, books of inspiration, and memes, of course. The story goes back to Zelda's parent, Carol Gardner. She was going through a deep depression fueled by divorce and debt when a four-month-old bulldog puppy named Zelda came into her life and kissed it all better. In an effort to follow her bliss (Zelda), she began dressing Zelda in human clothes, taking photos, and adding humorous quotes or messages inspired by them. Eventually, with help of photography by Shane Young, this turned into a '90s merchandising phenomenon called "Zelda's Wisdom" that continues to this day. And Zelda gives back by partnering with American Humane Association on its children's hospital initiative.

CITY DOG

What: *Zelda* statue

Where: Heathman Hotel, 1001 SW Broadway

Cost: Water is free!

Pro Tip: *Zelda* was sculpted by the brilliant Portland artist Jim Gion, who passed in 2018. His work is all over the city, from the zoo to Waterfront Park.

Anyhoo, in 2010, a life-size bronze sculpture of Zelda was unveiled to the city outside the Heathman Hotel. The Heathman wanted a way to promote the fact that they catered to dog-crazed Portland with special amenities. Not only can you stay at the Heathman Hotel with up to two doggies, but they will get their own pet bed, pet bowls, and a toy. They will greet your best friend with treats and a list of local pet resources.

Zelda *at her post outside The Heathman Hotel*

Getting back to the statue itself, *Zelda* sits sentry at the door, dressed in ill-fitting, beefeater doorman clothes. At her feet is a personalized water bowl that perpetually refills itself, bubbling water for all pooch passersby.

The real life Zelda was a guest on *Oprah* and *Good Morning America*.

THE CHAPMAN SWIFTS

What's the best air show in Portland?

When people want a suggestion for the best time to visit Portland, I'm tempted to offer up August, when most of the country is melting in extreme heat and we're generally enjoying blissfully moderate temperatures. But the correct answer is September. Because each September we get to celebrate the return of the Chapman swifts.

The location is the smokestack of Chapman Elementary School in Northwest Portland. Each September, 16,000 (yes, I've counted them) Vaux's swifts visit us on their way from Canada to Central America and South America.

If you don't know about these crazy birds, they roost like bats. In fact, they couldn't land horizontally like other birds, even if they wanted to. Often, they do this roosting in chimneys, which is why they are often called chimney swifts. But these particular swifts here in Portland prefer the smokestack at Chapman. The students have even adopted the swift as their school mascot.

THE RETURN OF THE CHAPMAN SWIFTS

What: Natural wonder/community event

Where: Chapman Elementary School

Cost: Free

Pro Tip: Bring a blanket to sit on and bring those binoculars that you always forget. Take the Portland Streetcar if you don't want to mess with parking.

The swifts spend all day hunting for insects, and then at sunset, they begin to gather in the sky. Like a mighty black cloud at first, they begin to swoop and perform. For approximately an hour, they put on an amazing show. And if you left before the finale, you'd still feel like you had seen something truly incredible. BUT STICK AROUND! After nearly an hour, they turn into a tightly grouped cyclone and shoot down the chimney with

A vortex of swifts gathering for the big event

impressive speed. I can't explain in any satisfactory way how cool it is to see this. Sometimes birds of prey show up to try and make a snack out of some of them, which is sad but also really exciting to watch. You can catch videos online but they fall pitifully short of the real-deal experience. And these birds do this every night for a month! Every year!

You'll want to arrive before sunset—maybe 8 p.m.—but come earlier if you want to beat the crowd.

If you have any questions, there are usually volunteers from the Audubon Society of Portland walking around who are just itching to talk about it.

UNA, THE PROFESSIONAL MERMAID

Would you like to pay a mermaid to swim with you?

Portland will not be pushed, filed, stamped, indexed, briefed, debriefed, or numbered. People try but people fail. The misanthropic, too-cool hipster? I would counter with Una the Mermaid. No city is more willing to let a magical mermaid swim or flop around openly without a snort or cynical scoff. Una is a mermaid, both personally and professionally, and everyone digs it. This particular mermaid holds a master's degree in conflict resolution, so even if you had a problem with her mermaidenhood, she could probably talk you down. Una's background includes adult education, child development, and restorative justice, as well as being a survivor of childhood trauma and family violence. All of this has led Una to a path of helping others heal and transform through creativity and imagination. She spreads mermaid magic free of charge to sick children, the disabled, the elderly, or anyone who is truly in need of it.

But make no mistake—Una is a professional mermaid and is happy to accept your human money to swim at your pool soiree or read stories at your child's birthday party.

Una also travels with her own 900-gallon tank if you'd like a live tank show at your event.

Photos courtesy of Una the Mermaid

One of Una's greatest legacies is the now annual Portlandia Mermaid Parade and Festival. Named in honor of our downtown's river goddess sculpture (by Raymond Kaskey), the parade is a grassroots event to celebrate the community's relationship with our rivers—and mermaids, of course.

PORTLANDIA MERMAID PARADE AND FESTIVAL

What: Grassroots celebration of mermaids and Portland rivers

Where: Tom McCall Waterfront Park

Cost: Free

Pro Tip: The last thing a mermaid wants is a polluted ocean, so try to use natural costuming materials if you're going as a mer-person.

OTA TOFU

Where can you get the best tofu outside Asia, and what does it have to do with World War II?

Portland has more vegan options than any city in the world. Most restaurants—heck, most saloons!—have quality vegan options. So it's no surprise that we have world-class tofu available here. But we're also home to the nation's oldest tofu factory and one that comes with a fascinating history.

Ota Tofu was founded way back in 1911 and it is still family owned. When the Ota family started their business, it was to provide a taste of home to the rapidly growing Japanese community. They cooked the blocks of tofu in gas-fired brick ovens, and though they catered only to the niche market of local Japanese, they did well. Until World War II, that is. I recount the Japanese experience elsewhere in this book, but the Ota family, along with tens of thousands of others along the West Coast, were taken from their homes and forced into internment camps. Most Japanese business owners either never recovered or had to rebuild from scratch. Amazingly for the Otas, four years later, they returned to find that a landlord had protected their location for them. They were able to start production again and serve an Asian population that had changed in their absence but not in its desire for that taste of home.

OTA TOFU

What: The nation's oldest tofu factory

Where: I buy mine at New Seasons, but you should drive by the historic building at 812 SE Stark St.

Cost: A couple of bucks

Pro Tip: If you're new to cooking with tofu, get extra firm and invest in a tofu press. It will change your life.

Ota Tofu, the nation's oldest tofu factory.

Eventually, the rest of the population began to appreciate the wonders of tofu. Even the Midwest, when I left it, was starting to come around a bit. And here on the West Coast, tofu is treated with the respect it deserves. As a near-vegan myself, I have eaten several tons of tofu. I know tofu. And Ota Tofu is hands down the best. Their handmade process, I'm told, makes the difference. All I know is that it is considered far superior to most other tofus, and owners who use it in the best restaurants and food carts agree.

You'll find Ota Tofu served at restaurants and food trucks all over the city and at local grocery stores like New Seasons and Green Zebra.

MADNESS!

Where can you see the severed ear from *Blue Velvet*, the knife from *Psycho*, and rent a copy of *H. R. Pufnstuf* from 1969?

Amazingly, you can see all of that in one single place, and it won't cost you anything unless you want to rent a movie. You can even watch a movie here for free. You can keep Disneyland because, for my money, this is the happiest place on earth. As a video rental store, it's maybe the best in the country, with over 80,000 titles (many impossible to find anywhere else) and staff members who know their business. You won't find a better selection of cult films, foreign films, or childhood classics.

Then, there's the museum. There are display cases all over the place, packed with amazing costumes and props from movie history. They have a Maltese falcon, for cripes sake! There are over 100 items on display; don't get me started. Go see it for yourself.

Movie Madness was founded in 1991 by Mike Clark. He bought his first piece of Hollywood memorabilia in 1995—the dress Diane Keaton wore in *The Godfather Part II*. Auction hunts and donations have built it to its current status. Mike retired in 2017 but wanted to see his vision continue. He approached another Portland institution, the nonprofit Hollywood Theatre (greatest theater in the world FYI), to see if they wanted to buy it. The

MOVIE MADNESS

What: Video store/museum/theater

Where: 4320 SE Belmont St.

Cost: Free

Pro Tip: They now host a film appreciation program, Movie Madness University, that meets in the miniplex. Go to hollywoodtheatre.org to learn all about it.

Left: *Prop from* Mars Attacks!

Right: *I pity the fool that doesn't know about Movie Madness.*

city came together and raised the more than $315,000 needed, ensuring Movie Madness's position as an irreplaceable cultural resource. Mike still owns the prop collection himself, but he has loaned it to the Hollywood and therefore to all of us.

There is the 18-seat Movie Madness Miniplex that shows cult classics and Saturday morning cartoons—FOR FREE!

YODA'S HOUSE

Where can I see the most Portland of homes?

I've heard this home referred to by many names: Hobbit House, Dome Home, Smurf House, and 'Shroom House are perhaps the most common. But having been raised on all things *Star Wars*, I immediately think of Master Yoda's house and then Luke Skywalker's home on Tatooine.

Whether it makes you think of hobbits, Smurfs, or mushrooms, this place is nuts. I first saw it and, of course, was impressed with its unique design, but then I learned that it was conceived and built by a *mime*! Pretty Portland, right? Francisco Reynders was a Dutch mime, actor, artist, and musician. He studied mime in Paris with Marcel Marceau and eventually moved to Portland to teach theater at Lewis and Clark College and work for the Portland Opera. He then opened the Oregon Mime Theatre, which was a big deal for a while and resulted in old Frans settling here for good and devoting six years to designing his dream house in 1972. He had spent years building sets and designing costumes for the New York stage, which perhaps explains the theatrical results.

Frans found these round turret shrouds in a salvage yard that turned out to be from a do we need to spell out World War II Essex-class aircraft carrier (the *Bunker Hill*). Some think they were actually domes built to test radar after the ship was decommissioned, but whatever they were, he picked them up

---

The main dome is about 30 feet around and 22 feet high. The insulation is literally full of Oregon history—Frans used copies of local newspapers.

The signature domes. Photo courtesy of Zillow.

for only 50 bucks. He was said to distrust corners and right angles, so this is just what he needed to inspire his home among the trees and perfect little creek. Those turret shrouds ended up being bedrooms and bathrooms—the holes where the aircraft carrier cannons poked out became skylights. Francisco's dream house ended up being nine domes in total, connected by a series of flat roofs.

DOME HOME

What: The Francisco Reynders Home

Where: 1850 Carriage Way, West Linn

Cost: Free

Pro Tip: The home has changed hands a few times since Frans's death in 1996. It's privately owned now, but the owners are kind enough to offer tours now and then and it's included on the Weird Portland Homes tour that happens every year.

THE ZYMOGLYPHIC MUSEUM

What the heck does zymoglyphic mean?

You probably remember from elementary school that zymoglyphic refers to those folk- art remnants from the region—I'm kidding; I have no idea. But artist Jim Stewart, who is responsible for the museum, provides this:

zy'-mo-glyph'-ic, adj. [Gr. zyme leaven + Gr. glyphe carving]

1. Of, or pertaining to, images of fermentation, specifically the solid residue of creative fermentation on natural objects

2. The collection and arrangement of objects, primarily either natural or weathered by natural forces, for poetic effect.

That clears it up, right? It is, in fact a made-up word, but then weren't all words made up at some point? The Zymoglyphic Museum is part museum of natural history, part art gallery, part carny sideshow, and part David Lynch movie—all of which are my favorite things. Here you will find dioramas and aquarium tanks filled with, um . . . curiosities. Stewart combines found objects (though sometimes bought or donated) with his artistic or spiritual vision to create unique pieces that look somehow genuine as well as fascinating. He has always been a collector: arrowheads, bird nests, marine animals, and the like. You can see this. There's an obvious wink from Stewart

---

There seems to be some world building going on here. Something connects the individual pieces and one gets the sense that, like Tolkien, Stewart sees the details of a world the rest of us are not privy to—right down to the stamps from the Zymoglyphic Post Office.

Many exhibits at the museum are watching you as well. Photo courtesy of Jeanne Kindbottom

here. You will find intentional humor. But there is also a genuine love—the love of a collector and the kind of love that puts fire to an artist's coal. Jim even hosts residency programs at his studio. Go see it. It's the size of a two-car garage, so it won't take all weekend. It's free and worth every penny.

IS THAT A SKINK PLAYING A GUITAR?

What: The Zymoglyphic Museum

Where: 6225 SE Alder St.

Cost: Free

Pro Tip: As of this writing, viewing is by appointment, so email zymoglyphic@gmail.com to find a good time for a good time.

RESISTANCE IS FUTEL

Is that really a working pay phone I just passed?

Probably not. A phone? Yes. Pay? No.

What you undoubtedly saw was the work of a group of volunteers called Futel. Futel is a perfect example of what can happen when organized public art meets public service. They look just like pay phones, and they are, in fact, created out of old phones and recycled software. The phones are fully functional, free to use, and even if you don't have anyone to talk to, you can pick up a Futel phone and they'll give you someone to talk to. You can dial one and talk to the mayor's office. Or you can hang around and wait for the phone to ring. Volunteers call randomly just to talk. They provide bus schedules, help lines, and anything that might be of public interest. If you dial zero, and a volunteer is available, an actual human operator will answer and help you.

Funded by donations and grants (mostly art-based grants), it is undoubtedly art of the performance variety. But the fact that these phones are located primarily in areas near houseless communities also makes it a true public service. The Futel phones even provide free internet access. Most of us take our phones for granted; however, there are many who don't have the ability to make a simple phone call whenever they want. And who knows how many people out there just need someone to listen?

FUTEL PHONES

What: Public art meets public service

Where: Visit the map of locations at futel.net/map.

Cost: Free

Pro Tip: Go to futel.net and help keep it going by buying a T-shirt.

Close up showing Futel Phone directions and information. Photos Courtesy of Futel

It's urban furniture. It's a comment on phones and the loneliness of modern technology. It's a comment on the economic gap. It's a social experiment. It's subversive and interesting, good for the community, and, not least of all, it provides anonymity and therefore gives the fun of prank phone calls back to the children of Portland.

Futel phones have even been used, at least once, to save a life via a 911 call.

THE FRIENDLIEST SCULPTURE IN TOWN

Where can you interact with art and simultaneously say hello to thousands of people at once?

The Fuller Road light-rail stop along the MAX Green Line will take you to the most charming kinetic sculpture you're ever likely to see. I love sculpture, but so much of it is cold or esoteric. It takes itself too seriously. That's why I love the work of Portland artist Pete Beeman. You've undoubtedly been to Powell's Books, so you've noticed his piece, *Pod*, right across the street. It's the one that has the bronze counterweight hanging like an uvula in the middle of three wheeled legs. You push the uvula and the steel cable hair swings back and forth. Beeman's art always comes with that spirit of fun that attracts even the art averse.

WAVING POLE

What: Kinetic sculpture

Where: The Fuller Rd. light-rail stop (Green Line)

Cost: Free

Pro Tip: Beeman has another piece at the Gresham rail stop called *Iris*, which you can also play with, works like a camera shutter, and lights up. Very cool.

Perhaps you see a many-winged bird, or multiple birds with the standard two wings, or a tree, or big yellow smiles, or the spinal column of Mechagodzilla; but the title is telling. It's waving. It's saying hello. A bright yellow howdy for everyone beyond and below.

The Waving Post. Courtesy of TriMet

His piece along the light-rail gets much less attention, which is why I wanted to put it in this book. Titled *Waving Post*, the piece is elegant, with its broad, bright yellow outstretched wings hinged symmetrically upon its red ribs and silver spinal column. But the real joy comes when you get up close and realize you can play with it. There's a crank at the base, and when you turn it, those wings wave to all the neighbors and passengers on the MAX and Interstate 205. How friendly is that? It stands 22 feet high and is abstract enough to be open to interpretation.

DINOSAUR FLIES

What is that crazy thing flying around that looks like a dragon, and will it kill me?

Those things are actually called "snake flies," and they're terrifying. If you didn't grow up seeing these things, you won't be able to believe that they exist and no one is talking about them. They have these long, worming necks, which is why they're called "snake" flies, but that's a terrible name for them. Sometimes, people around here call them "camel flies," which is way too cute a name for these crazy things. They should be called Satan flies or perhaps alien invasion flies. They look like something that will swarm the land after the apocalypse has finished with us. They are a w hole inch and a half long sometimes and have giant mandibles. Two long, membranous wings, veined and transparent, allow them to swoop down with terrifying speed. Large compound eyes on the sides of their heads enable them to study you and learn your weaknesses. Two long antennae twitch on top of their heads. My theory, if anyone wants to know, is that they are constantly transmitting information to the mother ship. Their publicists would like you to think that snake flies are considered beneficial because they eat aphids and

THE SNAKE FLY

What: Jurassic bug

Where: Anywhere you least expect them and in wooded areas (which are everywhere!)

Cost: Your blood—I'll never believe they don't bite with those giant mandibles.

Pro Tip: Snake flies are not actual flies of any sort. They're more closely related to lacewings, which is a lovely name for something that is also pretty creepy.

The Jurassic Snake Fly, preparing to strike fear into the hearts of Oregonians.

other pests. What they don't want you to know is that they have an adhesive organ on the bottom of their bodies that they use to glue themselves to vertical surfaces—like your face. Supposedly they rarely bite humans, but I'd shoo it off my arm if I were you.

They are, in fact, considered living fossils and are a leftover from the early Jurassic period.

ZOOBOMB PYLE

What is that stack of bikes over by Powell's–is that art?

Yes, it is! And no, it isn't! It started as a public service, from one biker to another, and has evolved into a full-on beloved local landmark—both artsy and fartsy. To understand it, you have to know what a Zoobomber is. At the turn of the 21st century, a group of minibike-loving funsters started gathering for group rides down a hill beginning near the zoo. That explains the "zoo" part of the name. The "bombing" part became accepted lingo due to the insane speed the riders would reach. Another label that arose was the Holy Rack, which was also known as a Zoobomb pile—a tower of minibikes anchored to a rack at their meeting point at SW 10th Avenue and Oak Street. These bikes were there for any riders who didn't have a bike. By 2006, the pile had grown up a bit and became the People's Bike Library of Portland. Anyone could use a bike for the price of a five-dollar ID card from the custodian known as Handsome Dave.

Another city would have shut this kind of thing down, but not Portland. We stepped it up. BikePortland.org got involved. They worked with the city and found $10,000 of the Portland Department of Transportation's money to put some big-boy pants on this thing and make a city-endorsed bicycle parking rack/art piece. *People's Bike Library of Portland* was designed by local artists Vanessa Renwick and Brian Borrello and installed in a traffic island at W Burnside Street and SW 13th Avenue in

PEOPLE'S BIKE LIBRARY OF PORTLAND

What: A functional work of public art

Where: Burnside and 13th

Cost: Free

Pro Tip: Just call it "the pile," and locals will know what you're talking about.

The Pile. Courtesy of Scott Beale/Laughing Squid laughingsquid.com

2009. Zoobombers didn't lose control of their baby, however. They collaborated to ensure that it remained a functional rack and still a "bike library" where people who need a bike can borrow one. That it is, but it is also a steel-and-gold-leaf sculpture, 17 feet tall, featuring a two-story, spiral-shaped pillar. A golden bicycle sits atop the whole thing—a glistening homage to Portland's love of biking.

The unveiling featured a ribbon-cutting event that included a speech from the mayor and a parade from the original Holy Rack to the new one by veteran Zoobombers, who also laid down the first bikes.

MONKEY PUZZLE TREES

What are those crazy-looking trees all over the place that look like dinosaurs?

Portland, being home to a rain forest, has a number of fascinating floras to discover. A trek into Forest Park, Tryon Creek, or any of the neighborhood forest trails around here will provide a Jurassic Park experience, with wild and ancient-looking plants, huge and contorted trees, slugs the size of compact cars, and more. But the monkey puzzle tree, like most Portlanders, comes from someplace else entirely—in this case, Chile.

The monkey puzzle tree is Chile's national tree, and it does date back to the dinosaur days, just like you'd think. It was the occasion of the 1905 Lewis and Clark Centennial Exposition that we have to thank for these dino-trees. A representative from Chile gifted some seedlings to Portland, and they were planted throughout the city. Some say that ship captains from South America also brought seedlings to sell at the fair.

JURASSIC FLORA

What: Monkey puzzle trees

Where: All over the city, but three from the fair itself can be found at 419 NE Hazelfern Pl., 415 NE Laurelhurst Pl., and 446 NE Fargo St.

Cost: Free

Pro Tip: Multiple online maps exist of monkey puzzle trees in Portland. Google "monkey puzzle tree map of Portland," and take your pick.

Even one of its leaves will live for about 24 years, so every generation has to rake the yard at least once in their lives.

So why is it called a monkey puzzle tree? The legend says that in about 1850, a wealthy Brit had acquired one for his garden, and upon seeing it, his pal Charles Austin remarked that even a monkey could get lost climbing it. Besides their lizard-like appearance, the trees can grow as tall as 130 feet. Their spiked pine cones can be eight inches in diameter. Like anything with this much personality, people tend to love or hate them. But the trees will outlive their enemies. They can live to be 2,000 years old.

SAUVIE ISLAND UFO

What's this I hear about a UFO crash-landing on Sauvie Island?

For years, I couldn't find the answer to what this spaceship-looking thing was or why it was sitting there, battered, abandoned, and dripping with moss. As it turns out, the UFO is actually an unidentified floating object—which is still pretty cool—and the story of its creator and his creation is worth the deep dive.

Richard Ensign was a navy civil engineer, sent to Princeton where he actually met Albert Einstein. Ensign had an aversion to the status quo and put stock in intuition and he had a near pathological resentment of waste, which coincided with his belief in helping others and his ingenuity, using unconventional materials. Decades ahead of his time, his own home was an experiment in quick minimalist structures that could be affordable to most. The Sauvie Island UFO was itself an experiment, not just in engineering, but with an eye to providing a way for people to achieve personal freedom using unconventional and easily acquired materials.

SAUVIE ISLAND UFO

What: The wreckage of an idealist's invention

Where: Sauvie Island, Collins Beach

Cost: Free

Pro Tip: Be aware that it does rest on the clothing-optional portion of Collins Beach, so if you don't want to potentially see a lot of flopping private body parts, give it a pass.

The boat was designed to house twelve. Ensign had learned about the versatility of cement while working for the Army Corps of Engineers, so cement became his material of choice. True to his ethos, Ensign invented and built his own equipment, which included a cement mixer made from a 50-gallon steel drum and a lawn mower motor. The entire structure consisted

Courtesy of Erik Gouger

of a rebar skeleton stuffed with cement and an interior sprayed with foam. It was envisioned as a floating house, complete with a wood-burning stove in the center to keep its occupants warm and to cook the fish they would catch from lines hanging over the sides. Ensign would work on perfecting his design for more than a decade.

Why is it sitting there? The answer seems to be the great flood of 1996. But Richard's son, Jon, says that the boat was sold and then moved against his father's advice—which led to it being sunk in some manner. Then the flood loosened it from its watery grave and washed it up on the shores of Sauvie Island, where it now rests.

You can explore this impressive saucer for yourself, just 10 miles north of Portland. The Sauvie Island Bridge will take you to the island and your ultimate destination: Collins Beach. You'll leave paved roads behind for a stretch, and when you see those brown signs with little numbers on them, park as close as you can to No. 3. Then hike down the trail a bit, turning right when you hit sand. Keep your eye to the woodsy bits and you'll see it sticking out less than an eighth of a mile down the beach. Visitors are able to explore all around it, and a makeshift ramp has even been added so that you can climb inside. You'll want to be careful, however, because this is a wreckage, not a government-maintained attraction, and you don't want to be the one who finally falls through the floor to your death—although that would add to the legend . . .

The craft has been tagged and ornamented with the work of street artists, but I think that would appeal to its creator—a man who placed a high value on freedom of expression.

PUIRKS—PORTLAND QUIRKS PART 1

What strange things do born-and-raised Portlanders not know is strange?

There are a plethora of oddities here that simply no one talks about. It's not that these are secrets exactly, it's just that those born and raised here don't know any different or take them for granted. It goes back to that fish who doesn't notice the water. But I not only notice the heck out of 'em, I also notice people *not noticing them*. I call these things PUIRKS (a portmanteau of "Portland" and "quirk"). There are hundreds of them, but I'll just name a few of my favorites because I've been dying to talk about them:

1. Dogs in Shopping Carts

Umm, why is there a German shepherd in this Walgreens?

I know Portland doesn't have a monopoly on loving dogs, but it truly is on another level here. Dogs are absolutely everywhere. People bring their dogs to work. And if you're looking to rent and you have two dogs? No problem in Portland. Nearly every place accepts dogs. You can probably bring your dog to that restaurant you're planning on going to tonight. Portland business owners know that allowing dogs is good for business, and besides, they brought their own dogs to work today, so . . . But really—dogs at the pharmacy and grocery stores? Yep! I'm told that this practice started because there is an Oregon law that deems it discriminatory to force those in need of a service animal to put one of those service

WAGGING TAILS AT WALGREENS

What: Dogs everywhere

Where: I'm talking EVERYWHERE

Cost: Free

Pro Tip: Okay, some places have signs on the door prohibiting dogs, but I'll bet you could take them to court and win.

animal uniforms on their dog and announce to the world that they have some medical issue. That was all Portlanders needed to encourage them to take their dogs to Freddie's for a carton of oat milk.

2. Cheerful People at the DMV

This one is really spooky. I have dealt with the DMV several times now, and everyone has been delightful. And here's the thing—they're really inefficient. You'll be in there for days. But the people there are wonderful. Helpful even. I can only assume they get paid truckloads of money. Or perhaps they're all high.

3. Same Thing at the Airport!

You ever had a cheerful TSA agent pat you down? You will here. I look forward to it happening again!

4. Sunbreak City

First off, it rarely rains here. What Portland calls rain is something else. Mist? Drizzle at worst. But even on most rainy days, blue skies poke out for a bit. I call them sunbreaks. My wife calls it peek-a-blue weather. People will argue with me about this but I'm correct and have never lied to you as far as you know.

Portland rains just five inches more a year than the average city, which doesn't even put us in the top 20 rainiest cities in the country.

THE WORLD'S LARGEST LAWN ZOO

Where can you visit amazing zoo animals without costing you your retirement fund and without the moral quandary of contributing to caging animals?

One of the few good things to come from the 2020 pandemic quarantine is the "A to Zoo" museum. The creative love child of artist and "public joy maker" Mike Bennett, this gift to the neighborhood sprang from a few big bummers. Mike came from Pennsylvania with a degree in art education and a desire to make a living with his art if he could. He made outdoor artwork with reclaimed wood and house paint and displayed it in front of his house. In April of 2020, just as the pandemic was getting its claws dug in, a lot of that artwork was stolen. Mike was bummed and began keeping his art inside. Neighbors, however, began reaching out and asking him to share his work again. His "giant wooden cutouts" had always been a joyful addition to the city, and with the pandemic closing everything down, people desperately needed things to do.

MIKE BENNETT'S LAWN MUSEUM

What: Public art/education

Where: Finding it is part of the fun. Currently, I can only tell you that it is north of Alberta St. It may move soon, so check mikebennettart.com to keep tabs on him.

Cost: Free, but Mike sometimes asks for donations to various causes.

Pro Tip: Mike likes to do scavenger hunts with his art as well, so follow him on all the socials for extra goodness.

Taking walks was one of the only activities left to us and Mike realized that he had a responsibility. So, armed with his training in education and art, he created the *A to Zoo Alphabet*

Courtesy of Mike Bennett

One of Mike's many signs around town

of Animals. And each morning, he would release a short video about the new animal and show his artistic process. People loved it! People needed it! His artwork is all over town now, having appeared in various educational and fun projects. His lawn museum is constantly growing and changing, so who knows what wonders will have been produced by the time you read this, but it will be inspiring and educational, and . . . did I mention fun yet?

Mike created 26 animals in 26 days—a new animal each day until he ran out of letters.

YORK: TERRA INCOGNITA

Who was York and why is there a statue of him at Lewis and Clark College?

I was failed by the public educational system. Raised in the St. Louis area, you couldn't spit without hitting a historical marker honoring Lewis and Clark ("On this spot in 1804, Lewis tied his shoes"), but I did not learn about York until I moved to the other end of the Oregon Trail. York, for those educated in the same whitewashed manner as I was, a Black slave who accompanied the Lewis and Clark expedition to the West and was invaluable to the venture. York was Clark's slave. The two grew up together, but that didn't make them friends because Clark was a racist. Still, Clark valued him enough to realize what an asset he would be on the dangerous venture. As a member of the team, York was allowed to do things slaves generally wouldn't have been able to do. He carried a gun, hunted, and was even allowed to vote on things like where the winter would be spent.

YORK: TERRA INCOGNITA

What: Sculpture

Where: The campus of Lewis and Clark College

Cost: Free

Pro Tip: The campus is the most beautiful campus you're likely to see, and worth a visit. Mount Hood overlooks LCC and offers a stunning view by the reflecting pool.

York was the first African American to cross the continent and get to the Pacific Ocean. And he thought when they returned as heroes, he would be granted his freedom. But while the other members of the team all got land, York got whipped for expecting a little respect and then probably sold.

York sculpture at LCC, courtesy of Jeanne Brawn

What happened next is up for debate. Clark told Washington Irving decades later that he actually freed York and set him up as a transporter of goods. But do we trust Clark? Nah. I prefer the version (as do many historians) told by a fur trader who says he knew York from meeting him in what would eventually become Wyoming more than once. York lived among the Crow Indians, who treated him like a chief. He lived well and had four wives.

About that statue, though—titled *York: Terra Incognita*, it stands on the campus of Lewis and Clark College. Charles Neal, who is African American himself, was introduced to York's story in a book recommended by a high school teacher and that spark became the impetus to get recognition for York. Neal was ultimately able to rally support and get the college (his alma mater) to partially fund the project. The rest came from donors like his schoolmate Jacqueline Alexander and her husband. The sculpture itself is powerful; it is the work of Alison Saar, an artist influenced by African folk art, which is on display here. I've visited York many times myself, and in the spring, you will usually find fresh-picked flowers at his feet.

Students and scholars visit Lewis and Clark College continuously to research the expedition, and York is there as a potent reminder of his important role in the history.

YES SURREY

Where can you bike along the river on a Surrey bike while helping provide services for children and adults with developmental disabilities and mental health challenges at the same time?

I see all manner of fun-looking bikes zipping around when I'm down on the waterfront, but only today did I learn about the good deed behind them. You've probably seen something similar in other tourist towns or perhaps at an overpriced amusement park run by a cartoon rodent. But at least two things make this bike rental special: it's a nonprofit, and they offer adaptive bikes so that anyone can take a spin, no matter what condition your legs are in.

They're called Kerr Bikes and all their bike bucks go to support an organization called Albertina Kerr. Albertina Kerr has been around since 1907, providing services for people with intellectual and developmental disabilities and mental health challenges. And those adaptive bikes I mentioned? They're part of a partnership with the Portland Bureau of Transportation and Nike called Adaptive Biketown, which grants greater access to bikes for people with disabilities. This includes hand-powered bikes, electric-assist trikes, and stable trikes with calf straps.

But getting back to that horrible dad pun of a title up there, they do rent two- and four-person Surrey bikes, complete with

KERR BIKES

What: Partnership between bike rentals and do-gooders

Where: Tom McCall Waterfront Park, 1020 SW Naito Pkwy., and at OMSI

Cost: Varies per bike and duration, but a two-person Surrey is $25 an hour.

Pro Tip: They even offer a free bike repair station for the waterfront—complete with tools, tire pumps, and a bike lift.

Courtesy of Kerr Bikes

fringe on top. And if you're not into the fringe benefits of the Surrey, there are plenty of others: deuce coupes, choppers, quad sports, and tandems. They also offer regular old adult and children's bikes for you people who always order vanilla.

THIS JUST IN! Kerr Bikes just let me know that they will be adding boats as well! Eight kayaks and four paddleboards will be available to rent for use on the waterfront by the time you're reading this!

TWIN PINES COUNTRY CLUB

What is the only country club in the country that would accept me and that I can afford?

Olivier Bouwman came here from the Netherlands in 2010, and it's hard to imagine him feeling as much at home anywhere else in this country. He must have felt the same way, because he picked Portland after exploring the US for a year in his VW camper bus. People love those camper buses here, by the way, and you'll see them everywhere. But I digress! Olivier is a software engineer by trade, but an artist at heart. He hits that sweet spot in the Venn diagram where science and art overlap. This has led to creations like his Glow Bunnies light sculptures, animated video walls, and small cubes with happy glowing lights inside that respond to touch.

TWIN PINES COUNTRY CLUB

What: Mini golf (Portland style)

Where: 8434 SE Clay St.

Cost: Free

Pro Tip: The name Twin Pines is derived both from the two pines on the course and the deep love of the film *Back to the Future* (Twin Pines Mall, remember?).

So, when he was faced with dead grass on his side lawn and simultaneously saw a notice on Craigslist for a large amount of free Astroturf, inspiration struck. He turned it into a free neighborhood miniature golf course. With six holes—complete with obstacles—the course is open seven days a week from

---

It is completely free to play and they don't even want your donations.

Photo courtesy of Olivier Bouwman

10 a.m. to 7 p.m. There is a windmill and statues of Dutch children, which were added to honor his homeland. Other parts of the world are represented as well: an Easter Island head and a Japanese pergola provide additional obstacles. A locker grants access to balls and clubs (call ahead for the code). If you go, respect the neighbors and keep the shouting to a minimum, will ya? You don't want to mess this up for the rest of us.

LOVE LOCK BRIDGE

How can I declare my love while I'm in Portland?

I've seen this trend in Paris, of course (okay, never been to Paris, but I did see a photo once); however, I didn't know it was a thing here in Portland until I came across it by chance. There is a pedestrian and bicycle path along the east shore of the Willamette River called the Eastbank Esplanade. A mile and a half long, it extends from the Hawthorne Bridge past two more bridges and ends at the coolest bridge of all time—the Steel Bridge. The Steel Bridge Riverwalk offers pedestrians and bicyclists a magnificent view of downtown, just about 30 feet above the Willamette River. And this is where the love locks began appearing several years ago.

The tradition is that a couple symbolically declares their "locked" love by literally locking a small padlock on the fence and tossing the key into the river. Although I am often an old grump, I think it's moving to look upon all of those manifestations of love. Portland city officials must too, because they let it happen even though it's technically a form of vandalism. I worry about all those keys in the river

LOVE LOCKS BRIDGE

What: Local landmark to declare your love

Where: Steel Bridge Riverwalk

Cost: Free

Pro Tip: There are plenty of public art pieces to enjoy along the Eastbank Esplanade as well.

If your love is not as unlockable as you thought, I'll rent you my bolt cutters for $20 so you don't have to think about that lock out there mocking you.

Ryan and Paige locked down their love in March '22. Photo courtesy of Jeanne Kindbottom

though. I hope fish don't eat them and get sick. If that's a thing, I guarantee someone will install a box for depositing keys. There will probably already be one there by the time you're reading this.

PUIRKS—PART 2

What are some more strange things that native Portlanders don't know are strange?

1. Water Stations

It may be my favorite thing about Portland that you don't have to ask for water here (and I'm just barely kidding about that). Nearly every place you will ever eat in this town has a water station and cups. You can serve yourself any time you want. You've just scarfed down six baskets of chips and salsa and you really don't want to ask the waitress for yet another glass of water? Not a problem here! Go help yourself to all the water you want. This is even true at concert venues. On occasions when I didn't want to drink beer at a show in St. Louis or Chicago, I'd have to stand in a long line and suffer the eye rolls of bartenders if I wanted to stay hydrated in the mosh pit. And then I'd generally get a small cup filled by that bartending hose with all the buttons, and it would taste like dishwater. But here, you will find water stations! No line! No eye rolls! Yet another reason I love it here.

MOSQUITO DROUGHT

What: Rare natural anomaly

Where: Everywhere. Or nowhere? No mosquitoes everywhere and all mosquitoes nowhere.

Cost: Free!

Pro Tip: We do, however, have slugs the size of surfboards, regular sugar ant invasions, and spider webs as big as bed sheets, if those kinds of things bother you.

2. Sugar Ants

The first six times I visited Portland, the places I rented had tiny ants all over the place. The managers said they'd never heard that before. When I moved here, the house I rented had swarms of tiny ants. The landlord said he'd never had that problem. Well, it isn't me! They're called sugar ants, and if you

Water station at Revolution Hall

crush them, they release a death stink that is supposed to smell sweet but you wouldn't mistake it for candy. It's an alarm to other ants and they will come running to help. So don't smoosh them. Nothing works. You just have to wait out the ant season; it will pass. Portland has an ant problem but no one wants to talk about it. I'll let you know if I get to the bottom of it.

3. Skeeters?

I don't know why this is not talked about, but there are no mosquitoes here. Okay, technically, they do exist here. People will tell you that they have them, but they don't know what they're talking about. They have mosquitoes here like most places have bats. Yes, they can be found here. And yes, if you go to specific places, you may even be likely to see one. But unless you live in a cave or a Transylvanian castle, bats don't impact your life. That's what it's like here with skeeters.

The lack of mosquitoes is due to the dry summers and year-round Pacific breeze.

MAD DOC RAVEN'S PLACE

Where can you get a mug of Grave Water and a burger (branded with a pentagram), served by a goblin?

I get this question all the time, and the answer is Raven's Manor, a new cocktail lounge in Portland with a haunted mansion theme. Legend has it that the joint once belonged to the unbalanced Dr. Raven, who performed unspeakable experiments with his many elixirs. And he liked to party. Long dead now, the dark souls of former partygoers, monstrous subjects of his experiments, and locals all lurk here regularly. Dr. Raven's journals with all his elixir recipes are here, and the mixologists behind the bar are masters of mixing them for you to try. Naturally, they will be poured from skulls and sipped from glass lab equipment. But make no mistake, these are serious drinks, designed by people who know what a martini should taste like, and the Grave Water, with its hints of grapefruit and rose water, is just as bright and delicious as it sounds.

Food? Yes, and they don't skimp here either. You can get light pub food like Graveyard Dip served with tombstone crostinis or good ol' fries and onion rings (oddly, no tater tots). Or you can fill up on heartier dishes like pasta and giant burgers if you don't mind the sign of the devil branded on your bun. Oddly for such an evil place, there are loads of vegan options. Portland!

Even better than simply grabbing a table or sitting at the bar, they offer parties where they'll help party guests create

---

Whether or not you turn into a frog, you'll enjoy the onion rings here.

Ghost toasts at Raven's Manor; photo courtesy of Madeleine "Maddog" Cooper

their own cocktail concoctions known as "elixir experiences." Guests choose their drinks or "potions" from the menu. They are given lab coats to wear (spattered in blood, but the lack of dry cleaning keeps prices low), and Dr. Raven's widow will lead them through the story of her dead husband. One group of guests will work with the others to find clues hidden throughout the manor that will ultimately lead to the dungeon where the potion-making will take place. Once guests have found the dungeon (with all of its torture devices still on display), they will meet Dr. Raven's old assistant, Dr. Creeps, who teaches guests how to create delicious potions with a better-than-average chance of catching on fire or exploding.

RAVEN'S MANOR

What: Haunted cocktail lounge

Where: 235 SW 1st Ave.

Cost: Free to walk in, and a glass of Ectoplasm will run you $10.50.

Pro Tip: This place is popular, so while reservations aren't required, they will take them and you should make one.

THE PORTLAND TROLL BRIDGE

Who's that trip-tropping on my bridge?

Trolls, as we all know, live under bridges and like to eat billy goats and occasionally people. But this is Portland, baby. Our trolls are happy to see you: they are smiling wide with wild, colorful hair and plastic jewels in their belly buttons. The Portland Troll Bridge at 16498 NW McNamee Road is yet another favorite form of vandalism. The vintage troll dolls began appearing under the old railroad trestle in the early 2000s, but no one has been able to tell me exactly when or why. I've heard that somebody's cool mom hammered a couple of the dolls under there to surprise her kids. I like that version, so that's the one I'm going with. People in the area saw it and began adding their own. On any given day, you could see dozens or hundreds of trolls down there.

TROLL BRIDGE

What: A bridge. With trolls beneath it.

Where: 16498 NW McNamee Rd.

Cost: Free

Pro Tip: It's over by Cathedral Park and Sauvie Island Bridge, so add this to your itinerary when you're going to see the glorious St. Johns Bridge.

Be sure to bring a troll of your own to add to the collection, or there is a slight chance you may be eaten.

Beware the trolls!

Some people hate it, of course. Those troll dolls come with strong reactions ranging from "They're so cute!" to "Get those ugly things out of here!" Sometimes people in that last camp come along and purge the bridge of its horrible troll infestation. We don't like those people. Before you go, caveat emptor: those troll haters might have been there recently and left nothing interesting to see.

THE SECOND-OLDEST TIKI BAR IN THE COUNTRY

Where can you sit in a darkened roadhouse from the 1800s and sip an authentic mai tai?

My work as an illustrator attracts tiki people. If you dig my painting of Uncle Charlie from *My Three Sons* or my *Ghost and Mr. Chicken* ouija board, you understand the appeal of sitting in a really deep booth among sculpted lava, bamboo, and black-lit bikini babes, sipping on a zombie that is so authentic and powerful that they limit you to two. Nostalgia? Kitsch? Polynesian culture? Rum and sweet citrus and more rum? I don't know the fundamental source of the attraction, but if you dig it, you dig it. I dig it. And I'm glad to have a recommendation for the tiki lovers in my orbit.

THE ALIBI TIKI LOUNGE

What: Second-oldest tiki bar in the nation

Where: 4024 N Interstate Ave.

Cost: A traditional zombie is $13

Pro Tip: If you're going to order the scorpion bowl, you'd better bring a couple of friends and a designated driver.

Roy Ell, who bought the old roadhouse in 1947, was digging it before almost anyone. He was a navy veteran who fell in love with the South Pacific during his

The Alibi (minus Max now) is the real deal, having changed virtually nothing in all this time—save the addition of karaoke and an expanded menu.

Courtesy of Jason Moore

service and decorated his new place with all the Hawaiian art he had picked up during his life. Called Max's Alibi, it became only the second tiki bar in the nation. Tiki bars became big for a bit, but most died off with disco. Then there was a resurgence in the '90s, but they were fakers! Poseurs!

SLAP TAGGIN'

What's with all the stickers?

Visitors to any of Portland's busy streets cannot help but notice that our sticker game here is top notch. Many consider us to be the number one hub in the world. Within the last decade or so, we've established an international reputation for our sticker art scene. Artists from all over the world visit to add their contribution to the street gallery. To some, this guerrilla art movement on the backs of street signs, telephone poles, and utility boxes across the city looks like nothing more than thoughtless vandalism. But that would be missing the rich culture that stands behind the "slap tagging" movement. Also referred to as sticker slapping, sticker tagging, and sticker bombing, the art movement has been growing since Shepard Fairey slapped his way across the country with his "OBEY" stickers featuring a simplified portrait of Andre the Giant that got so much attention in the '90s.

STICKER SLAPS

What: Street art

Where: Everywhere one can stick

Cost: Free!

Pro Tip: Alberta is the best street for stickers that I've found, though art appreciation is subjective, of course.

Sometimes, they can justifiably be looked at as a subcategory of graffiti, but more often, at least in Portland, they rise to the level of street art—sometimes political, sometimes a comment on a social issue, sometimes humorous or simply aesthetic. You'll see the best in each category on our streets. Why is this particular art scene so prominent here? It probably goes back to the strong DIY culture that exists here and the fact that Portland is a city that respects both art and people's right to express themselves. The prevalence of makerspaces and a strong art community means that, regardless of income, most

Stickers on Alberta

artists have access to some kind of printer or press. Sometimes you will come across what is known as a Label 228, which can be a name tag or type of sticker used by the post office that can be picked up for free. But more often, the artist has gone to some trouble to produce the best version of their public art piece.

> Like other traditional street art, recurring characters and themes can be seen from one end of the city to the other.

JAN BRADY WATERFALL

All the tourist books have beautiful photographs of Multnomah Falls, but what if you don't like crowds?

Multnomah Falls is totally worth the short drive from Portland, and you will undoubtedly want to include it if you're visiting Portland for the first time. Get that photo. Climb to that little bridge and patiently wait for your turn to look over the railing. It is the Marsha Brady of Oregon waterfalls. But it's not my favorite.

My favorite, the overlooked sibling to Multnomah Falls, the Jan Brady of waterfalls, is Latourell Falls. It's right around the bend from Multnomah Falls and is its superior, in my opinion. First of all, although it can get a bit crowded on certain days, it isn't as densely populated at all times as Multnomah. Second, it drops straight down from its basalt cliff. Even the mighty Multnomah meanders a bit and tumbles around, but not Latourell. It really has a satisfying, thunderous gush. You can feel it in your gut, and the spray hits you in the face. Third, if you've got proper shoes and an

LATOURELL FALLS

What: Underrated waterfall

Where: Along the Columbia River Gorge

Cost: Free

Pro Tip: Wear a raincoat so you can get right up to the falls and feel the power all that water generates.

Behind the falls is this magnificent, cave-like amphitheater of blackened basalt. It was formed from slow-moving lava that cooled really fast. It's accentuated with vibrant green lichen that truly makes for a spectacular experience.

Left: *Mother and son in front of Latourell Falls*

Right: *The blackened basalt provides a dramatic backdrop.*

adventurous spirit, you can go right up to this waterfall. You can actually stand behind it, which is really amazing—mainly because of my fifth and most important reason for it being at the top of the list: the columnar basalt formations.

THE GREAT WILLAMETTE BOAT OF ILL REPUTE

Who was Nancy Boggs and can I spend the night in her floating brothel?

The fact that brothels populated the area in the late 1800s is well established. They were all over the Wild West with Portland being the Wildest and the West-est. And governments, being governments, were all in favor of it just as long as they got paid—at the very least in the way of liquor taxes. Now, you might expect bordello operators to love paying taxes, but Nancy Boggs did not.

What's important to know about this story is that Portland was three different cities at the time: East Portland, Albina, and plain ol' Portland. Bordello Boggs had the great idea that if she ran her business out of a barge in the middle of the Willamette River, she couldn't be taxed by any of the three! Also, she could serve all three cities and really rake it in. And without paying liquor tax, she could offer cheaper drinks. She would send an employee (let's call him Bordello Bob) out with a little boat that would shuttle clientele back and forth.

THE FULTON HOUSE BED-AND-BREAKFAST

What: Possible remains of a floating brothel

Where: 7006 S Virginia Ave.

Cost: Check thefultonhouse.com for rates

Pro Tip: Just a block from Willamette Park, with a rooftop deck on which to sip spirits and maybe even encounter the spirit of Nancy Boggs herself. Probably not.

Nancy did a great business. All three cities would try to raid her bordello barge at various times, but since, at any given moment, someone from at least one of the three police forces was partying there, she always got tipped off in time to steer to one of the other cities' shores in time to keep the party afloat. This worked great! But eventually, these three governments

Photo of the riverfront at the turn of the century

got tired of Nancy Boggs siphoning off their local businesses and, in turn, their tax revenue. With money to be made, the three normally contentious governments acted together and hit her from all sides. But Nancy was ready! She warded them off with a fire hose of scalding steam that was somehow attached to—well, I'm not going to pretend to know how boats work. But it was a successful retaliation and the coppers retreated!

However, later that night, someone (legend has it that it was a religious zealot who hated a good time) cut the anchor loose and sent the bordello barge racing down the turbulent river towards the ocean. Nancy tried to wake Bordello Bob, but he was drunk, so she jumped into the rowboat herself and found the captain of a paddle steamer and his crew who were willing to rescue the pleasure cruiser for the special thank-you that brothel owners were sometimes known to offer.

Eventually, Nancy got tired of the hassle and went (somewhat) legit by buying a proper bordello on Pine Street and paying her taxes.

So what happened to the original floating bordello? If the owners of the Fulton House Bed-and-Breakfast are to be believed, they have it. It was lifted from the water, dragged by horses to its current location, and used as the bones for its current incarnation.

MOST GORGE-OUS VIEW (SORRY, NOT SORRY)

Where am I going to get the best view of the Columbia River Gorge?

The guidebooks are going to send you to the Crown Point Vista House, an observatory, museum, gift shop, and rest area that sits above the gorge just 25 miles from Portland. Designed by architect Edgar Lazarus in the style of German Art Nouveau, it is a beauty and does offer an impressive 360-degree view of the Columbia River Gorge. You should check it out if you haven't.

But the view itself takes second place to that same vista from Portland Women's Forum State Scenic Viewpoint. It's just a tiny park (no bathroom or gift shop), but offers an unmatched opportunity to take in the best the gorge has to offer: Cape Horn, Hamilton Mountain, Little Hamilton Mountain, Beacon Rock, Mount Defiance, Angel's Rest, and Vista House itself, perched magnificently to the right.

Why is it called Portland Women's Forum State Scenic Viewpoint? It doesn't exactly roll off the tongue, but we have this group to thank for access to this stunning view. In 1950, a member of the Portland Women's Forum named Gertrude Glutsch Jensen reported at one of their meetings that loggers and mills were destroying the beauty of what she called the "Great Gorge of the Mighty Columbia River." The group rallied, raising money through doll shows, tea parties, fashion shows,

---

Once known as Chanticleer Point (and still called that by some locals), it was once the site of a log cabin inn that burned down in 1930.

View from the Portland Women's Forum Viewpoint

and donations. By 1956, they were able to purchase 3.7 acres at Chanticleer Point, eventually turning the land over to the State of Oregon "reserving to the Portland Women's Forum the right to erect and maintain a memorial on the property."

PORTLAND WOMEN'S FORUM VIEWPOINT

What: The best place to see the gorge

Where: Along the Historic Columbia River Hwy.

Cost: Free

Pro Tip: If you can take the very slight detour on the way to Vista House, then you can continue along the road to the waterfalls.

STARK NAKED ON STARK STREET

Is that topless female cyclist I just passed breaking the law?

Nope! It may seem strange to those of us who grew up in other parts of the country, but Oregon has very lenient laws pertaining to nudity. Basically, the law boils down to this: you can be naked, as long as you're not having too much fun or trying to turn anyone on. If someone is having any kind of sex in a public place, they are breaking the law. But if they are journaling or raking leaves while naked? Not a problem. However, this is a state law. Cities and counties can make up their own laws about it. So, in the actual city boundaries of Portland, for instance, it is not allowed to expose genitalia in a public place if there are members of the opposite sex present. But what about that woman on the bike with her top off? Breasts are fine. Not a problem.

Which brings us to one of the most beloved Portland traditions: the World Naked Bike Ride! This event is massive. We're talking in the neighborhood of 10,000 riders. Portlanders love their bicycles, and by June, when the ride takes place, Portlanders are so blissed out by the presence of the sun that they are ready to take it all off and celebrate. You will witness fully naked, partially naked, naked except for a Viking helmet . . . everything goes. And yes, it is legal. But why? Because it is officially deemed a protest (to highlight the vulnerability of cyclists and vehicles that pollute), it is protected under

---

The Sun Rovers are a Portland nudist group and a resource for clothing-optional events.

Sign at Collins Beach "clothing optional" area

Oregon law. But Oregon law still dictates that sexy naked time is a private matter. No public hanky-panky allowed on Naked Bike Ride Day. Drunkenness is also discouraged. Cameras at the start and finish line are prohibited, and participants are supposed to stay clothed until they get to the starting point. And, of course, being creepy is not allowed and will get you reported, tossed from the event, and maybe even arrested. Yes, the police are hanging around, along with medical professionals and bike mechanics—all fully clothed in case of emergencies.

What about that nude beach you've heard about? Why is that okay? Collins Beach is just outside of the city, so it goes by its own rules. Which means full-on nudity! Still, even at the nude beaches (there's one other, in Rooster Rock State Park over in the Columbia River Gorge), Oregon state law applies—no hanky, no panky, and no being creepy.

PORTLAND NUDITY

What: Wearing your birthday suit

Where: Collins Beach, Rooster Rock State Park, or on your bike with 10,000 other birthday suits

Cost: Free as a bird

Pro Tip: The northern end of Collins Beach is supposed to be "family friendly," but nudists wander over that way all the time so you've been warned.

PATHS TO INNER PEACE

Want to take a relaxing walk and yet go nowhere?

There's so much to do around Portland that it's easy to forget how important it is to quit doing and start *being*. That's one of the primary ideas behind walking a labyrinth. The attention to path occupies your right brain (or left, according to some; I don't have a horse in this race) enough to distract you from your thoughts.

You won't find them advertised, but Portland has some great walking labyrinths. For sheer elegance, you can't beat the one found at the Grotto. It is a copy of the medieval cathedral labyrinth of Chartres, France. I believe it's about half the size of the original, but impressive nonetheless. On the more organic side, there is the stone-and-grass labyrinth behind Mount Tabor Presbyterian Church. The church welcomes everyone and hosts a group walk as part of the church's TaborFest celebration in the fall.

The Unity Center for Spiritual Growth has a stone labyrinth located in front of its church right next to the parking lot.

At the Cedar Hills United Church of Christ (corner of Cedar Hills Boulevard and Park Way) you can find a pea gravel labyrinth surrounded by trees and gardens—a nice, quiet place for reflection, including a bench and a water fountain.

Looking for an indoor experience?

UNWINDING BY WINDING AROUND

What: Walking labyrinths

Where: Various locations around the city

Cost: Free

Pro Tip: Warning: the labyrinth on Sauvie Island is located on the "clothing optional" part of the beach, so you might encounter a nude volleyball game en route. That's either a positive or a negative, depending on how you roll.

Labyrinth at Collins Beach

First Christian Church at 1314 SW Park Avenue has a modern labyrinth in a classic medieval Chartres style painted on the floor. You can arrange to see it by calling the office at 503-228-9211.

The Peace House (2116 NE 18th Avenue) offers the only oval labyrinth I've seen. It sits right off the street, done in pavers, and they invite everyone to drop in and give it a try. A really lovely labyrinth sits in the Min Zidell Healing Garden at the National University of Natural Medicine. Call 503-552-1776 or email nagel@ncnm.edu to visit.

Finally, the simplest natural labyrinth can be found just north of Portland at Sauvie Island's Collins Beach. It's just beach rock and sand, but the mighty Columbia River roars on the horizon. To find it, park at sign No. 6 and walk left. You'll find it tucked away just where the land rises to a bit of a crest.

Labyrinths can be found in most spiritual traditions, from this land's indigenous communities with their Medicine Wheel to the the Celts and the infinite circle to Judaism and the Kabbalah . . .

BIKE LANE ART INSTALLATIONS

What's the story behind the awesome modifications to the bike lanes?

Creativity really does exist everywhere in this city. If there's a canvas, Portlanders will express themselves. It's difficult to find one of those people icons on street signs around here without the addition of plastic googly eyes at the very least (if not a dress and cowboy boots). The bike lanes here are no exception, of course, and I like the story behind it. It goes back decades to a city employee named Todd Roberts.

BIKE LANE ART GALLERY

What: Public art project

Where: All over the city

Cost: Free

Pro Tip: Portland Bureau of Transportation (PBOT) tweets out pictures of new artistic additions.

Back in 1999, it was Todd's job to lay down those thermoplastic stick-figure cyclists in the bike lanes. Either out of a desire for artistic expression or a streak of anarchy running through his blood, he took a triangle piece of that thermoplastic and gave his stick figure a hat. He and his coworkers expected their boss to get upset, but the supervisor didn't take the bait. "Looks good," he said. And with that stamp of approval, more artistic additions were born. Stickman's head was turned into a skull as a statement against drunk driving at the location of a fatal car accident. Todd added flames to the back wheel of a rider near a federal building. A stickman braving a bike lane that crisscrossed a highway was given a lucky horseshoe to hold. There were a cowboy, a witch, and a pony-tailed rider with a cigarette hanging out its mouth.

Other city employees joined in the fun. The legend goes that as the artwork came to the attention of city higher-ups, they

Bowie bike lane portrait

were (in Portland fashion) cool with it, as long as they remained family friendly. That is to say, no private body parts. Otherwise, have fun with it!

The following year, the metaphorical paintbrush was handed to Kirstin Byer, who had just recently retired as supervisor at the Signs and Pavement Markings Department. Under Kirstin, the art project left its rebellious roots behind and became a fun art project/gift to the city's bikers. Generally, the adornments have been geographically significant—a rider near a library, for instance, is reading a book and wearing a backpack. A rider near a golf course is carrying a bag of clubs. Some are truly impressive. There's one dedicated to Prince on East Burnside and Ninth Streets that wears a purple cape with the elaborate Prince symbol on it and a cloud above him with a cascade of purple raindrops. There's a David Bowie on SW Broadway with a guitar, surrounded by stars.

The project has become so popular that there is even an effort to get children into libraries with the "Bike to Books Contest." Children are invited to submit their designs for a chance at having PBOT's striping crews install their vision.

A MUSEUM THAT REALLY SUCKS

Want to see a collection that's just collecting dust?

I'm speaking, of course, of the Vacuum Cleaner Museum. It's housed within Stark's Vacuum Cleaner Sales and Service, so you can walk out with a brand-new Hoover after paying homage to the way things sucked in the past.

Here, you will find over 300 models of vintage rug suckers. Most of them have been donated by benefactors who were themselves bequeathed with one of these antiquated appliances. It makes sense. You can imagine any of these really fascinating and sometimes beautiful contraptions being passed to the next generation, who have no idea what to do with them. You can't find bags for a '46 Electrolux—believe me, I've tried. And closet space is pretty valuable these days. This conundrum has resulted in Portland's gain.

THE VACUUM MUSEUM

What: Just what you'd think it is

Where: Stark's Vacuum Cleaner Sales and Service, 107 NE Grand Ave.

Cost: Free

Pro Tip: Yes, you're walking into a vacuum store, but no one is going to hassle you to buy anything.

Marvel at wooden models that date all the way back to the 19th century! Though they are really more of what my mother

My favorites here are the space-age models from the 1960s. Those retro-futuristic designs look like something out of a *Flash Gordon* comic strip.

would have called a "sweeper," one of those motorless crumb munchers patented by Melville Bissell in 1876 is nothing more than a cylindrical brush in front of a dustpan on wheels. The real star here, however, is the "Busy-Bee," which required two people to operate. It was assumed that the man would pump while the wife did the actual vacuuming, and it is probably safe to say that this led to many fights. They say money is the cause of most arguments between couples, but I think it's joint housework and therefore the reason you've never heard of the Busy-Bee.

THE PORTLAND PICKLES

Where can you actually have a great time at a baseball game, even if you don't like baseball?

I'm not a sports guy. I don't like the money, the egos, or the boredom that comes with professional sports. They kicked me out of the Midwest for not watching every single sporting event available, but Portland doesn't care what I like and what I don't. The irony is, I kind of like sports again now that I'm here because they do it correctly, which is to say, remembering that games are supposed to be fun. The Rose City Rollers are discussed elsewhere in this book, but we also have the Thorns, who not only seem to win a lot but whose games are fun and full of ridiculous camaraderie in the stands. The Timbers have Timber Joey, who revs his chain saw and slices off a slab from a giant log every time the Timbers get a goal then presents it (them) to the goal scorer(s) in a postgame ritual.

But for me, a Portland Pickles game provides the most fun to be had at a sporting event. First of all, tickets start at $7 and end at $13, which takes the pressure off getting your money's worth, but I guarantee you're gonna have fun. The true spirit of baseball lives here. *Willamette Week* called them "*The Sandlot* meets *Oliver Twist*" because everyone involved really loves the game and because players from out of town are without home and family and generally stay with host families like foreign exchange students. These families get paid in season tickets, so, like, a hundred bucks. Money isn't dirtying things up anywhere down the Pickle line. It's literally all fun and games.

Don't miss Toss-a-Pickle Night, Karen Night, Tattoo Tuesdays, the Dude Night (free rugs to tie the room together), and, of course, Exploding Whale Night.

THE PORTLAND PICKLES

What: A collegiate woodbat team

Where: Walker Stadium at Lents Park

Cost: $7–$13

Pro Tip: Watch your beer because when the Pickles score, everyone with a chair that isn't nailed down will raise it over their heads and shake it with glee.

The Pickles are a collegiate woodbat team. They play at Walker Stadium, which is small enough that it only takes up part of Lents Park, where it sits. The team pays rent to the city to play there, and they also clean up after themselves. When it's not Pickles season, anyone can play there. How'd they get the name? Portlanders voted online. We could have been the Portland Pliers. We were very nearly the Portland Mud Hounds. But the right name won out and was announced at Woodstock Elementary School. The mascot is Dillon T. Pickle. What does the "T" stand for? "The," of course.

The beer and cider are cold, and of course they serve pickles. The games themselves feature all manner of ridiculousness and events.

GHOSTS AND GARLIC KNOTS

Where can you have a slice and maybe sit next to the ghost of a prostitute?

Well, the answer to that question may be, "A lot of places," but I know of one in particular—Old Town Pizza and Brewing. A pizza place may not typically conjure fear and dread (unless they use a Provel cheese product like they do in St. Louis), but Portland's favorite ghost hangs out at Old Town Pizza. Her name is Nina, and it's not pronounced like you think. As with Couch Street (pronounced "Cooch"), saying it wrong will mark you as a noob. It's pronounced "Nine-uh." But since there's no record of her, I don't see how we can be so sure. Regardless, Nina is the name given to the specter who floats among the pepperoni fumes, dressed in a long black gown, tapping people on the shoulder, whispering in ears . . .

OLD TOWN PIZZA AND BREWING

What: Hauntings and pizza

Where: 226 NW Davis St.

Cost: Garlic knots are just four bucks!

Pro Tip: Willem Dafoe hung out here all the time in the '70s, which is reason enough to go, but they also offer haunted tours of what may or may not be Shanghai tunnels below the restaurant.

The place used to be part of the Merchant Hotel, a fancy-pants place in what was known as the Old North End in the 1880s. And like most great hotels of the time, they had more prostitutes than Gideon Bibles. The legend is that Nina was one of these, and perhaps a victim of white slavery. She wanted out of the trade, so when a traveling missionary offered to help her if she gave information that would help shut the sinful place down, she agreed. Soon after, she was found dead at the bottom of the

elevator shaft, her name carved in a brick where she lay. Today, that brick can be found in a cozy booth at the rear of Old Town Pizza. Did the legend spring up to explain the name on the brick found during renovation, or was the brick carved as a warning to would-be squealers?

Does Nina really remain there, marking her presence with perfume as many guests insist? Go see for yourself. At the very least, they have amazing garlic knots on the menu, so you won't be disappointed, even if she doesn't show up.

THE FREE PITTOCK VIEW AND ORIENTATION

What is the best place to take in the whole city while standing in one place?

Pittock Mansion isn't exactly a secret. You'll find it listed in every Portland guidebook, I would imagine. But that's because of its historical significance and because of its impressive gardens. The Pittock Mansion was built for Henry Pittock and his wife, Georgiana, when they emigrated from London in 1914. Henry was the publisher of the *Oregonian* (still a daily, local newspaper and the oldest continuously published paper on the West Coast). The home is considered a French Renaissance–style château, but it had all the cutting-edge modern attributes available to the wealthy at that time: an elevator, a central vacuum system, a walk-in refrigerator, and an intercom system. As for the formal gardens, they were Georgiana's pride. She was an avid gardener and more fond of roses than your average person. She was an original founder of the Portland Rose Society, hosted the first Portland Rose Show, and was instrumental in creating the Portland Rose Festival. As you might expect, the mansion has some impressive roses hedging the joint.

PITTOCK MANSION VIEW

What: The place to view the whole city

Where: 3229 NW Pittock Dr.

Cost: Free

Pro Tip: If you're feeling powerful and want some exercise, you can trade the drive up to the mansion for a hike up the Wildwood Trail in Forest Park.

Those are great reasons for checking it out. But the generally unmentioned reason to visit Pittock Mansion is for the

View from Pittock Mansion grounds

unparalleled view. It sits atop a cliff overlooking Forest Park and the entire city. When I first visited Portland, I mentioned to a local that I had a hard time orienting myself because of all of the winding roads and dead-end streets. He told me to make the climb to Pittock. “It’s the place in Portland where you can really see it all laid out,” he told me. “You can see the rivers, the mountains, the highways, and the streets. It’ll really help you get the hang of the city.” So I did, and he was right! On a clear day, you can even see all the mountains.

If, like me, you are directionally challenged (understatement in my case), I suggest you make the drive up to Pittock. The view is free, beautiful, and educational.

DR. TONGUE'S I HAD THAT SHOPPE

Where can you go find all the things your mother threw away?

I have a theory that toys held more importance for my generation than all others. We had the most latchkey kids. We walked home from school to an empty apartment, tore into a box of sugar bomb cereal or cold Pop-Tarts, then entertained ourselves with toys and television until someone showed up to make us dinner. Then it was back to toys in our bedrooms while the parents complained to each other about their day and watched the news. We simply had so much face time with our toys that when Gen X kids walk into Dr. Tongue's, they're likely to have a Rosebud moment and start crying. Maybe that's just me. Maybe I'm oversharing.

DR. TONGUE'S I HAD THAT SHOPPE

What: Vintage toy and treasure shop

Where: 7129 NE Fremont St.

Cost: Depends if you're going to buy that *Six Million Dollar Man* lunch box or not

Pro Tip: Featured on *A Toy Store Near You* Season 4 on Amazon Prime

And don't get me wrong—I've seen children in this toy store as well, having a blast. But the real magic happens when the grown-ups come in and see the Bionic Woman doll they had as a child or the Aurora monster model they always wanted. Spend some time here and I promise you will hear "I HAD that!" more than once. I said it myself 27 times last Saturday.

Dr. Tongue's is lovingly curated by Mark Pedersen, and he's been dealing in collectibles most of his life. His first shop, Dr. Tongue's 3D House of Collectible Toys, closed in 2005 but rose

Army of Ultramen. Photo Courtesy of Dr. Tongue's I Had That Shoppe

from the ashes in 2015 in a new location. Mark knows his stuff. I asked him about what turned out to be a little Cracker Jack toy, assuming he wouldn't have much to say about it, and he knew where the factory was in Mexico and that the molds still existed! You'd expect a guy running a place like this to know his *Star Wars* collectibles (he does), but c'mon! Mark was a monster fan like me, so you'll find plenty of vintage monster toys, models, and *Famous Monsters of Filmland* magazines. He also sells reproductions as well as some midcentury knickknacks and vintage tiki-themed items. If that sounds random, it isn't. It all fits somehow, because if you're the kind of a person who likes the *Six Million Dollar Man* doll and drools over a *Dark Shadows* board game, you probably also like that set of tiki glasses over there.

If you're looking for something, looking to sell something, or just want to talk about Evel Knievel toys, chat Mark up—he knows absolutely everything and is a hell of a nice guy.

PUIRKS—PART 3

Why are there only four cans in the six-pack I want to purchase at this gas station?

1. Canarchy!

This isn't strange to Portlanders, but to most of us it is complete anarchy! You see, it is perfectly acceptable here to bust open a six-pack or twelve-pack of your beverage of choice and purchase the number you want. It costs more that way, but you can do it. Occasionally, there is a sign saying that you cannot do it, but otherwise? Go for it. I haven't done it myself. I can't bring myself to do it. It feels so wrong.

Another thing that will totally confound my fellow Midwesterners and most Westerners (the South has its own complicated liquor laws, but you expect that kind of thing when you're in Bible City, West Virginia): I call it *Portland's game of hide the hard liquor*. Here's the thing—you can get beer and cider and cocktail mixes at the grocery store. Oh, and wine. That's not a problem. You can also purchase these at gas stations and drugstores. But if you want a "spirit," you have to go to a designated "liquor store." In a societal flip, you can buy weed on nearly any block in town, but liquor stores are actually pretty scarce, comparatively. That seems random enough, but what's really strange to my Midwestern upbringing is that liquor stores don't sell beer! What?! I won't bore you with too many details. It's all about separate licenses, and taxes, and (I suspect) the Oregon Liquor and Cannabis Commission lining their pockets, blah, blah, blah . . .

As of this writing, you can only get that Costco crate of Grey Goose if you drive to Washington state.

Filbert "gravel"

2. Hazelnut-Flavored Gravel

Do you know how many of the country's hazelnuts are grown in Oregon? *All of them!* I'm not kidding. One hundred percent of all US hazelnuts come from more than 1,300 Oregon farms. Only Italy and Turkey combined grow more than we do. It's our state nut. But in Portland, they're called "filberts." And because we have so many filberts around here, people have discovered uses for them beyond Nutella sandwiches. In Portland, they use them for ground covering on paths and parks and playgrounds. Where the rest of the world would use gravel or bark, Portlanders use hazelnut shells. It isn't normal, but they think it is. I asked a man selling bags of shells at a farmers market about it. He explained that beyond being prettier, they also keep out slugs, snails, and cats. They also retain moisture in the soil and reduce weeds. But, of course, he was trying to sell me a bag of hazelnut shells, so . . .

STRANGE BOOZE ROOLZ

What: Breaking up six-packs and other weird behavior

Where: Everywhere in the city

Cost: Extra gas and high-priced hard liquor

Pro Tip: Go to John's Marketplace in Multnomah Village for the best selection of canned libations.

THE WITCH HOUSE

What's the real story with that creepy house in Forest Park?

You may have heard of the Witch's Castle, a truly witchy-looking, crumbly, moss-covered structure tucked away in a corner of southern Forest Park. If Portland were any other major city, there would be some kind of historical plaque there, telling the public all about its history. But Portland doesn't play like that. Tourism happens, but the city's not going to try too hard.

It was, in fact, a house at one time. A man named Danford Balch lived there with his wife and nine children (poor, poor woman) in 1850. He hired a man named Mortimer Stump (a name I didn't make up, believe it or not) to help him work the land. Mortimer apparently did not read the fine print of his contract and thought it would be okay to start a relationship with his employer's fifteen-year-young daughter, Anna. Papa Dan didn't like that one bit, and so when Mortimer and Anna ran off to elope, he thought it would be okay to get drunk and put a bullet in Mortimer's skull. The authorities disagreed with Danford's style of disciplining his employee, and he was arrested and hanged. The history I read stated that this was the first legal hanging in Oregon, which makes me wonder about all those less-than-legal hangings.

Danford's wife, Mary Jane, was now queen of the castle for many years. Then the place was absorbed by the government and used for everything from a park ranger station to a hiker's

---

Some say the place got its nickname because Danford blamed the murder on the bewitchment of his wife. I like that version better. Forget what I said about the stoner kids in the '80s.

Photo courtesy of Kim "Dabitch" Van Patten

WITCH'S CASTLE

What: Local legend and landmark

Where: Lower Macleay Trail

Cost: Free

Pro Tip: Park at Upper Macleay lot and follow the markers for Stone House, the building's official (boring) name. It's only about a 15-minute hike.

restroom, until a storm nearly finished it off. Decades later, a different species of Mary Jane came to dominate the dwelling when partying teenagers discovered it as a perfect place to . . . be teenagers. This was the 1980s and the height of satanic panic among lame adults, so this creepy-looking stone edifice, covered in vines and surrounded by forest, naturally became known as "Witch's Castle."

DARCELLE XV

Which way to the oldest living drag queen?

Darcelle XV (a.k.a., Walter Cole) was named in the 2018 *Guinness World Records* as the "oldest working drag queen." Before the pandemic shut down the city in 2020, Darcelle was still working at age 90. As of this writing, Darcelle is still performing six shows a week. If retirement finds Darcelle by the time you're reading this (never!), the Darcelle XV Showplace will certainly continue. It's the oldest continuously running cabaret in the United States and the showplace Darcelle has owned and headlined for well over 50 years.

THE DARCELLE XV SHOWPLACE

What: Nation's oldest drag queen's palace

Where: 208 NW 3rd Ave.

Cost: Varies depending on the show

Pro Tip: They will do company parties, so tell your boss.

Walter was born in 1930, served in the army during the Korean War, settled down with a wife and two kids—all the things a man of his time was "supposed" to do. He bought a coffeehouse, which eventually included a basement jazz club. Being an integral part of that scene must have helped Walter experience a world less concerned with society's norms. In 1967, Walter bought a tavern in northwest Portland called Demas (eventually

---

In 2020, Darcelle XV Showplace was officially recognized as a national historic site—the very first location in the state to score that honor based solely on its contribution to LGBTQ history.

Photo of Darcelle courtesy of Sarah Mirk

to become Darcelle XV Showplace). By '69, Walter had left the closet and his wife, and introduced the city to Darcelle (a nod to French actress and singer Denise Darcel). The 1970s brought success, as Darcelle XV Showcase became "the" place for cabaret and drag.

Could the self-described "four-eyed sissy boy" with "a crew cut and horn-rimmed glasses" ever have imagined how legit he would one day be deemed by his hometown? In 2011, Darcelle received the Spirit of Portland Award and was named grand marshal of the Portland Rose Festival's Starlight Parade.

SHE WHO WATCHES (*TSAGAGLALAL*)

Where can one see true petroglyphs along the Columbia?

A short drive from Portland will take you to the Dalles—a city named by fur trappers after their French word for "gutter." It was the location of a brutal, stony gorge that made their lives difficult. Locals pronounce it *dalz*, by the way—one syllable—but don't forget the "the," because that's part of the name as well. And thereabouts you will find a stretch of river valley that separates Oregon and Washington. This area was a traditional gathering place for the Yakama, Umatilla, Nez Perce, and Warm Springs tribes.

SHE WHO WATCHES

What: *She Who Watches* petroglyph

Where: Columbia Hills Historical State Park

Cost: Free

Pro Tip: Due to the risk of defacement, you must have a park escort to see *She Who Watches*. Call 509-439-9032 to set up a free tour.

But in the '50s, the federal government began the Dalles Dam Project to produce hydroelectric power, which produced rising waters that completely changed the valley, ruined tribal fishing, and generally made bad things worse for the descendants of the original caretakers of that land. The tribes rightfully protested that the precious rock art, the petroglyphs, would be submerged. Of course, that didn't

---

The petroglyph is called *Tsagaglalal*, or *She Who Watches*, in the Wasco-Wishram language.

She Who Watches *petroglyph*

stop the project, but they were able to save over 40 individual petroglyphs by jackhammering them out of the cliffs and putting them in storage.

Now those pieces of tribal art are back in nature, in a permanent display at Columbia Hills Historical State Park. Most can be seen from the walking trail: thunderbirds, deer, fish, owls, and—the most interesting—a strange tentacled creature. But the real treasure, *She Who Watches*, painted in red ochre, is perched high in the cliff. The legend is one of a female chief who watched over her tribe from the cliff above, always concerned for her people and what might happen to them when she was gone. A coyote told her that the time of female chiefs was coming to an end and turned her to stone so she could watch over the land for all eternity. There are other interpretations, I'm told, and there is debate about whether the coyote was tricking or helping. They're wily, those coyotes.

JERRY, PATRON SAINT OF SOUTH WATERFRONT

Why is that beaver over there wearing a silly hat and surrounded with flowers?

One of the most popular walks in the city is the trail along the South Waterfront, near the foot of the aerial tram. Along this trail, you'll pass along the cove of Cottonwood Bay, worth seeing if you really dig trees, as this is one of the few remaining stands of cottonwood trees on the west bank of the Willamette River. But the real hero of this trail lies just past the trees—*Jerry*, Patron Saint of South Waterfront and the Heron Pointe Wetland. *Jerry* is a three-foot-tall, bronze beaver. He stands watch over the Heron Pointe Wetland, a tiny riverine habitat right in the city. He is not officially named at all, but Portlanders have come to call him *Jerry*—as in Jerry Mathers, as in the Beaver from television's *Leave It to Beaver*. *Jerry* might be a girl beaver, however. I can't tell on the actual animal much less on a bronze statue.

Hang out by *Jerry* for a minute and you'll notice that nearly everyone pats or rubs his head as they pass. And *Jerry* is almost always being honored in various ways. You'll find him adorned with flowers, either placed at his feet or in his little hands. He is often wearing a hat, Mardi Gras beads, or a costume to fit the season. Sometimes he's holding an inspirational sign.

Mike Houck deserves his own book, but you should know that he is the force who persuaded Portland Parks and Recreation to turn Oaks Bottom into a wildlife refuge in the

---

There are other more impressive sculptures to be found in the city, perhaps, but none more lovable than *Jerry*.

Gotta keep Jerry *safe in these pandemic days . . .*

AS THE BEAVER

What: Public art

Where: South Waterfront walking trail

Cost: Free

Pro Tip: Place a coin at *Jerry*'s feet and you will almost certainly experience better-than-average luck for 24 hours.

'80s, using guerrilla tactics when necessary. He is also the hero of Heron Pointe Wetland, *Jerry*'s home. Developers didn't want to save it. They deemed the less-than-one-acre wetland too small to worry about. But Mike, some other activists, and the Audubon Society of Portland won the day. Condos lie just behind, and one of the tenants, Lucy Wells, commissioned the beaver statue to memorialize her late husband.

THREE GROINS IN A FOUNTAIN

Can we talk about that giant, white marble sculpture in the fountain?

Do you love it? Hate it? Love to hate it? I guess I'm in that last camp. What we have here is a sculpture designed by Count Alexander von Svoboda (a fake sounding name if I ever heard one). It was carved from a single 200-ton block of white marble that was quarried in Greece. That's impressive! That ought to be cool! It is not, but I love it.

Installed in front of the Standard Insurance Center in 1970, it sits a few blocks down from Pioneer Square on 5th Avenue. The sculpture depicts five people, floating around in the buff—three women, a man, and a child. The artist, Count von What's-his-name, claims that it represents man's eternal search for brotherhood and enlightenment. You're not likely to get that when you're standing in front of it, or on the way home either. It made some people mad at the time because,

THE QUEST

What: Hilarious public art

Where: Pioneer Square at 5th Ave.

Cost: Free

Pro Tip: Beloved Portland author Chuck Palahniuk writes about this statue in *Fugitives and Refugees*, which is reason enough to visit the silly thing.

Despite the clever nickname (lost on you if you've never heard of the song or movie "Three Coins in a Fountain," there are actually five figures here. A child and another woman are hidden behind the three prominent figures.

The Quest, *photo courtesy of Jason Moore*

you know, naked. But most people I know are just amused. There's something so silly about it that locals don't call it *The Quest*. They call it Saturday Night at the Y or Three Groins in a Fountain. I love it when citizens rise up and rename something. It's like when I was a kid in Chicago: everyone referred to the food joint Dog n Suds as Arf n Barf.

VELKRISTAN'S NIRVANA

Where would you suggest an inhabitant of a gwome visit while in Portland?

This is an easy question to answer, for Portland is blessed to be the very location of Velkristan's paradise! There's even a historical plaque to mark the holy place. Of course, only the pure of heart can see the place itself, but that probably describes you, so no need for concern.

For non-gwomes, perhaps I should explain *Kcymaerxthaere*, a global work of multidimensional storytelling. Geographer-at-large Eames Demetrios travels the world (and there are plans for the moon) installing bronze plaques to commemorate historic events and places from a parallel world within our linear world. He has described *Kcymaerxthaere* (or *Kcy*) as a novel of sorts, with its story's pages placed here and there and everywhere. I am reminded of Lewis Carroll's "Jabberwocky" when it comes to *Kcy*. It makes no sense and much sense all at the same time.

VELKRISTAN'S NIRVANA

What: Historic location

Where: 2100 block of NE 10th Ave.

Cost: Free

Pro Tip: I am not really that pure of heart, but I could still see the plaque. Just sayin'.

The first plaque was placed in Athens, Georgia, in 2003. Since then, another 141.5 installations have been set up in what we, in this universe, would call countries. That ".5," by the way, represents the future moon installation, which I have no doubt will happen. Demetrios already has placed one 12 meters below water off the coast of Bali. That one, "The Life of Bala Qhova," tells the story of Bala Qhova, famed for being the first to domesticate the water mole.

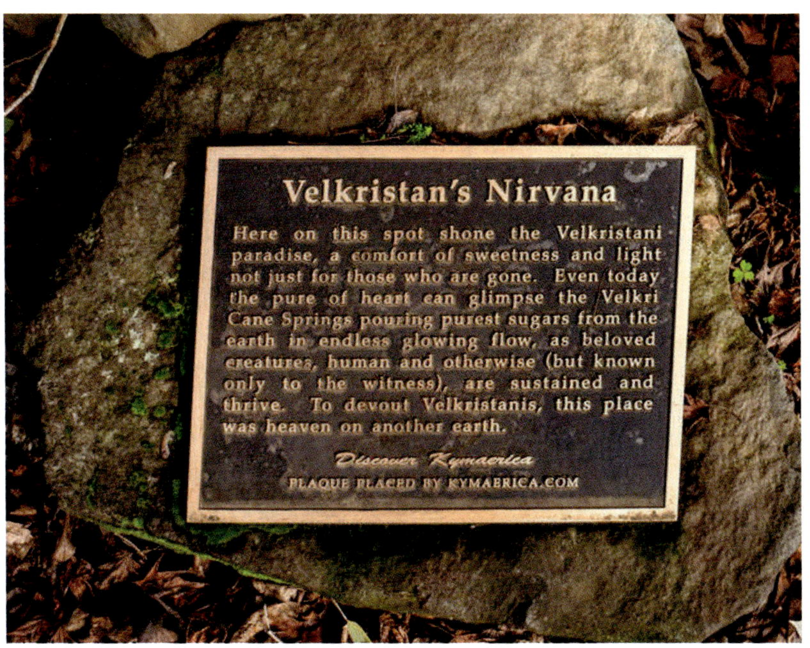

So, what does Portland have to offer in the way of *Kcymaerxthaere* lore?

Something pretty special, and the marker can be seen on the 2100 block of NE 10th Avenue. The geographer states: "This plaque honors an extraordinary place, visible only to the pure of heart. Some Velkristanis believe that springs are the densely compacted essences of the Columbia and Willamette (Stanklyk and Wilhamenta, respectively, to them) rivers, which disappeared upon merging, once allowing the sea to flow to Portland."

Demetrios is the grandson of midcentury design legends Charles and Ray Eames, which makes total sense, and is also an artist, author, and filmmaker.

A GAME OF BRUTAL BEAUTY

What's the greatest athletic organization in the city?

The Rose City Rollers, our local Roller Derby champions, are out to smash and destroy any remaining stereotypes about women athletes, as well as any preconceived notions about what an athletic organization can accomplish. The RCR is a flat track Roller Derby league, a founding member of the Women's Flat Track Derby Association, and a 501(c)(3) nonprofit organization. They dominate the track, but their declared mission statement gives a better taste of what they're all about: "The Rose City Roller's mission is to serve women, girls, and gender-expansive individuals who want to play the team sport of roller derby, connect with an inclusive community, and realize their power both on skates and off." To that end, they partner with organizations helping reach underserved populations like Brown Girl Rise and Active Children Portland. They offer scholarships, they lend gear, they run programs for youths (Rose Petals) and juniors (Rosebuds) as well as a recreational program

ROSE CITY ROLLERS

What: Kickin' Roller Derby nonprofit

Where: The Hangar at Oaks Park

Cost: $7–$20

Pro Tip: Roller Derby in the '50s was often scripted like wrestling, but that's not how it goes down now. They play for real and an elbow to the face will send you to the penalty box.

If you've never been to a Roller Derby event, the RCR's tagline, "A Game of Brutal Beauty," truly sums it up.

Rose City Rollers

known as the Wreckers. They are truly on a mission and the city is much richer for it.

They are also a hell of a lot of fun to watch. They have a home season that runs from January to June featuring their intraleague teams: Break Neck Betties, Guns N Rollers, Heartless Heathers, and High Rollers. They travel year-round, however, with their all-star, interleague team, Wheels of Justice.

WOODY WOODPECKER'S LAUGH

What do the halls of a Portland high school have to do with Woody Woodpecker?

The greatest voice in the history of cartoons, Mel Blanc, grew up in Portland. He was known, of course, as the voice of Bugs Bunny, Yosemite Sam, Daffy Duck, and dozens of other Warner Bros. characters. He was also Barney Rubble. But to me, his greatest contribution was voicing the original Woody Woodpecker. Woody became cleaned up and civilized over the years (devolution), but the original Woody Woodpecker of 1940 was absolutely insane. He was drawn that way and Mel Blanc voiced him that way—a psychotic bird way out of his tree and in desperate need of Thorazine. That trademark laugh was the sound of insanity in Blanc's artful hands (or rather, vocal cords).

He recounts in his memoir that he had that maniacal laugh in his arsenal, all ready to go when the opportunity arose. He had perfected it, as it turns out, in the halls of Lincoln High School. You can imagine the kind of student he was, and his memoir backs it up. He was the class clown and almost certainly had ADHD, with an emphasis on that H. He was easily bored and couldn't keep still. He changed his name at age 16 (from Blank to Blanc) when a teacher told him he would amount to nothing and end up like his last name: blank. He loved to do those voices, which

BIRTHPLACE OF WOODY WOODPECKER

What: Lincoln High School

Where: 600 SW Salmon St.

Cost: Free to walk around

Pro Tip: Other notable alums include Matt Groening, Elliott Smith, and Nate Query of the Decemberists.

Mel Blanc, photo courtesy of pdxhistory

included imitating his teachers, of course. His shoes were worn from all the trips to the principal's office.

Mel tells about the birth of Woody's laugh at Lincoln. It seems the acoustics of those empty halls were a canvas he could never ignore. He thought he was alone one day and tried perfecting an insane laugh he was working on. But alas, the principal was lurking there and was not even slightly amused. Mel's explanation about the halls' great echo and refining his art didn't help. "I should kick you out of this school!" the principal exploded. But Mel managed to hang in there until graduation and stuck around Portland for a bit after that. He had a regular gig performing on KGW radio on a program called *The Hoot Owls*, at age 19. Hollywood eventually called, but he never forgot his hometown. He supported the local Portland charity Neighborhood House throughout his life.

Mel Blanc credited growing up in multilingual South Portland as the source of his interest in voices.

TWILIGHT SWAN HOUSE

Did you know you can actually stay at Bella's house?

My daughters absolutely love those *Twilight* movies—you know, the ones with Kristen Stewart and Robert Pattinson where the vampires are all dreamy and glitter in the sunlight? Now that they're in college, they pretend to love them ironically, but we all know that's a lie. Despite my efforts to raise my children with proper knowledge of vampire lore by viewing Universal and Hammer movies from olden times, they did not escape the teen romance tarpit of the *Twilight* franchise. So when we moved to Portland and discovered that Bella's house from the movie is just a jaunt over to St. Helens, we had to go take pictures immediately.

Little did we know that very soon, the house would be available to rent as a vacation property. The quaint little house went up for sale in 2018 and was snatched up by a fan (as it should be). Amber and her husband Dean considered living in it, but opted for restoring it to closely

THE *TWILIGHT* HOUSE

What: Bella's actual house from the *Twilight* series

Where: 184 S 6th St., Saint Helens, Oregon

Cost: $396 a night

Pro Tip: Even if the house is already booked during your stay, the riverfront is lovely and worth the trip for *Twilight* fans.

The 2,000-square-foot house, built in the 1930s is a short walk away from the historic riverfront and central to all of *Twilight*'s PNW filming locations.

match the décor from the movie and rent it out. You can dine at the actual table from the film, sleep in Bella's bedroom, and basically run around acting out the movie.

THE GOLDEN WEST HOTEL

How did a Black middle class hotel manage to rise in the super racist early 20th century in Portland?

As of this writing, the Golden West Hotel is being considered for the National Register of Historic Places. The building at Northwest Broadway and Everett is not architecturally distinct enough to earn the honor, but its history will almost certainly get the Golden West its due.

By 1905, the transcontinental railroad was recently finished, Union Station had just opened, and the city had just celebrated the Lewis and Clark Centennial Exposition—all of which resulted in a flood of visitors (and therefore workers). The railroads hired a lot of Black workers, but Oregon, to its eternal shame, was legally a Jim Crow state and there were no hotels for a person of color. The only option was to find a Black-owned boarding house, of which there were very few, or flop with family or friends.

THE GOLDEN WEST HOTEL

What: Historic landmark

Where: 707 NW Everett at Broadway

Cost: Free

Pro Tip: An exhibit featuring six panels and a soundtrack can be seen and heard by the public on both sides of the Golden West Building.

Enter the Golden West Hotel. The hotel was built by rich white people and intended to be sold to some other rich white person, with only white guests. But the project was too ambitious and came up for sale just when the nation was struck with financial disaster. Also, the area was quickly becoming a Black community. It was sandwiched between the two most prominent Black churches in the city, the Bethel AME Church and the Mount Olivet Baptist Church. The hotel fell back under the control of the bank.

Photo courtesy of Ian Sane iansane.smugmug.com

William Duncan Allen was a brilliant Black entrepreneur from Tennessee, and he saw the hotel as a potential for investment. He leased the building and created the only hotel for Black people in the city. It opened in 1906, offering 100 rooms and quickly becoming much more than a place to sleep. It was a cultural hub. It hosted several Black-owned businesses including a gym, a Turkish bath, a barbershop owned by Waldo Bogle, and an ice cream parlor: A.G. Green's Candy Shop. Families would flood the place after church, prominent Black entertainers and politicians visited the hotel, and civil rights hero A. Philip Randolph stayed there. Freddie Keppard's Original Creole Orchestra played at the Golden West in 1914, which may have been the first official jazz concert in the state.

The success of the hotel brought backlash from the white racists, of course. The *Oregonian* newspaper claimed it was a brothel and wanted it shut down. To be sure, prostitution, illegal drinking, and gambling took place there, but so did women's clubs, family dinners, and charitable functions. As a microcosm of an entire population, it was home to everything you would expect to find in any community. The Golden West Hotel stayed in business until the Great Depression. But the building survives, looking very much the same from the outside as it did in its heroic heyday.

The Golden West is one of our most important landmarks and stands as a testament to the brave people who overcame horrific persecution to form a community of their own—to not only survive but thrive.

THE MOST LOVED CARPET IN THE WORLD

Why do I see people taking pictures of the floor at the airport?

Okay, this goes back to 1987, when it was decreed that a carpet be laid down in the Portland airport to reduce the noise of all those feet. Every other lame airport of the time was going with a boring earth tone. A company named SRG Partnership came up with something they felt captured the true spirit of the Northwest. Teal! And if that wasn't modern enough, they designed geometric shapes of lavenders and red that would represent the intersection of the runways that the air traffic controllers would see from the tower at night. The result was so '80s, you can almost hear Duran Duran just by looking at it.

Was it "totally tubular" or "gag me with a spoon"? Yes. Like Duran Duran, you could make an argument either way. But also like Duran Duran, the carpet inspires deep nostalgia. Really deep. People began taking pictures of their feet on the carpet and posting them to social media. The extent of this carpet love was not fully realized until the overlords decided to replace the now worn-out carpet in 2013. People went nuts. Their youth was being taken away. The carpet's pattern started showing up on T-shirts and hand towels. Trail Blazer point guard Damian Lillard released an Adidas sneaker with the awesome carpet design. When the ripping

BELOVED CARPET

What: Famed airport floor covering

Where: PDX

Cost: Free unless you want to own a piece of the old carpet, in which case, prices vary.

Pro Tip: Go ahead and take that mandatory picture of your feet. Everyone understands. But don't do it in the middle of traffic. Stand to the side, will ya?

of hearts and carpet began in 2015, the event was marked with a ceremony including airline employees and a swarm of media. Local retailers began selling pieces to the public.

Amazingly, the new carpet was not shunned or spat upon. Perhaps because the new architects, Zimmer Gunsul Frasca Partnership, were part of a Portland organization, the feelings of its citizens were taken into account. While the teal necessarily had to bank more toward green, the design looks pretty similar. The new geometric design now reflects both natural and man-made shapes around the airport and looks less like a video game. We're now supposedly looking down at airplane wings, hiking trails, leaves, and waterways. People felt that the designers were certainly trying to honor their childhood, and since the floor covering was made with recycled carpet, bottles, and jars, it was recognized as quintessential Portland.

Interestingly, on the very day I wrote this, the airport announced that the iconic carpet design would be returning upon the opening of a new terminal in 2024! Woot!

SPUD PUPPY PASSION

Is it just me or does this town have an unnatural love for tater tots?

Most of us who did not grow up in Portland have a different relationship with tots. We had them in our cafeteria lunches. They were not crispy. They were limp, kind of damp and cold, and far from delicious, but we were glad to see them. It was more a comment on the state of the cafeteria lunches than our feelings about tater tots. We were equally glad to see that glue-topped, tomato-paste bread that they called pizza. There were a very few places where you would see tater tots in the wild. Most fast food places only served fries. But when they turned up, it was an exotic treat and you would order them, no question.

So when I first came to Portland, it didn't take long to notice that tater tots are absolutely everywhere. They are in fast food places, food trucks, bars, and bowling alleys, and even high-priced, cloth-napkin places have them. They get all Portland with them here and fill them with other food like peppers, bacon, onions, and pineapple; they even roll them around in aioli, Oaxacan cheese, and spicy fish sauce. I had to find out why, because these are the kinds of things that plague me when I should be working.

My research has turned up a few things that gave me an answer I can live with. First of all, tater tots were born here in Oregon. The Grigg brothers got in on the ground floor of the postwar frozen food boom. Their factory was on the border of Oregon and Idaho, which led to the company name: Ore-

---

The most Portland of tots have to be the Spicy Fish Sauce Tots at Bottle Rocket (1207 SE Hawthorne Blvd.), garnished with crushed pistachios and mint.

Nephi Grigg, tater tots inventor

Ida. They were doing great with frozen corn, but the big bucks were in french fries so they got a tater-cutting machine. But it had a problem. Irregular potatoes would result in some bits and pieces that were not fry worthy. So they found a machine that would separate that starchy middle bit from the undesirable ugly bits. But Nephi Grigg, having grown up in the Great Depression, didn't like waste, so the brothers figured out a way to smash those bits and form them into little spud barrels. A salesman from Ore-Ida traveled around the country playing a ukulele and raving about what he had called "tater tots." There you go! So they're local!

The other part of the story seems to belong to bars and strip clubs. We have always had a lot of both and if you sell booze in Portland, you have to offer food as well. Food magically soaks up all the booze and prevents drunks from walking into traffic. And some of that food has to be "hot"; beer nuts are not enough. And what's the easiest hot food to make? Tater tots, of course. Fries really need to be fried (it's in the name), but tots can be baked and still be terrific.

A TOWN OBSESSED WITH TATER TOTS

What: A lot of tots

Where: Everywhere, even church

Cost: $6

Pro Tip: Tatchos? Yeah, Portland invented those, too.

RIMSKY-KORSAKOFFEE HOUSE

Where is the scariest place to get an absolute killer dessert?

The locals call it Rimsky's because it's easier. And you're not likely to hear about it unless a local introduces you to it because they have weird hours, do business out of an unmarked Victorian house in southeast Portland that you're unlikely to pass on accident, and don't advertise. The desserts are made in-house, and they are outstanding. So is the coffee. But that's not why you've come. You've come for the unique atmosphere.

The owner, Goody Cable (which is just what you want her to be named), insists that the joint is haunted by the previous tenants who were both writers and lived through the Russian Revolution. The dimly lit, ephemera-laced atmosphere is described as "casually threatening," which is spot-on perfect. I've heard it called a "haunted Victorian brothel," which also nails it. The tables are all named after composers, and live classical music adds to that "threatening" ambiance. Why is

RIMSKY-KORSAKOFFEE HOUSE

What: Haunted coffeehouse

Where: 707 SE 12th Ave. (at Alder)

Cost: About what you'd expect for dessert and coffee

Pro Tip: The name itself is a joke—a pun of sorts on the name of Russian composer Rimsky-Korsakov, but you knew that.

Use the bathroom while you're there. I'm not legally allowed to say any more on that subject.

One of the many surprises at Rimsky's, photo courtesy of Jason Moore

classical music so frightening? It's not as scary as singing children, but still . . . If all that hasn't sold you on the place, some of the tables rotate slowly, or suddenly rise, or shake. If you ask for water, someone from the kitchen will come out and squirt you with a water pistol. Bring cash. This place doesn't exist in the 21st century and you don't want it to.

CRIMING IN STUMPTOWN

Is there really a system of underground tunnels beneath Portland, constructed for the purpose of shanghaiing sailors?

The stories of the Shanghai tunnels are gumbos of fact and fabrication—blended so thoroughly that you'll never pull the ingredients apart again. Some facts are not in dispute. Shanghaiing sailors was certainly a thing here in Portland. Shanghaiing is that particular brand of kidnapping referring to sailors taken against their will and used as slave labor on boats, though the term "crimping" seems to be the term used most often. A crimp was a person paid to procure these sailors by any means necessary.

The late 19th century was the golden age for crimping, when wheat was in big demand overseas. Captains were responsible for replenishing their crew in any way necessary, and the crew had a habit of disappearing after a long Pacific voyage without Netflix or women. So they turned to unscrupulous crimps who had a few favorite plays: beating a drunk unconscious, slipping a drunk a Mickey Finn (chloral hydrate), or grifting. The most sophisticated went like this—a crimp (often in league with a hotelier or saloon owner) would find drunk sailors and offer them a comfy place to sleep, a great meal, some money to gamble with, maybe a prostitute . . . all on credit.

TUNNEL TOURS

What: Portland Underground Tours

Where: Old Town, 131 NW 2nd Ave.

Cost: $23 for adults/$19 for seniors and youths 11–17/$9 for children 5–10

Pro Tip: Sheltered parking available nearby at the SmartPark on NW 1st and Davis St.

Illustration of a "crimp" in progress

Then, under threat of police or worse, the sailors would be forced onto ships to serve off the debt they couldn't possibly pay.

And the tunnels? The tunnels existed but were probably not often used for crimping. They were unnecessary. Carrying a drunk sailor to a ship would hardly have been a shocking sight. Besides, crimping was legal as long as you played by the rules. These ships were owned by wealthy businessmen who profited from crimping, so international law ensured it stayed legal all the way into the first part of the 20th century. And often, the victims were homeless or transients, so local governments were just as happy to be rid of them. Crimpers knew not to slip a Mickey to a "respectable" member of society.

But tunnels were very useful for other criminal activity. Chinese merchants built tunnels to smuggle opium. And tunnel systems were handy for the owners of illegal gambling and drinking establishments who needed a quick getaway for themselves and patrons in the event of a raid. And if the tunnels were beneath these kinds of places, and these are certainly where crimpers would find their victims, it isn't hard to imagine that the tunnels could have been used for that purpose as well.

Can we visit these tunnels today? Any tunnels leading to the river would have been demolished when the riverfront seawall went up in 1928, along with the buildings there. But the remnants that remain beneath Old Town are available to visit.

A business called Portland Underground Tours claims to give you the real deal, and you're certain to hear some great Portland outlaw history.

A GREAT TIME WITH SOME STRINGS ATTACHED

Where can you get a bit of history that isn't boring and also a free puppet show?

The best museums are ones that are labors of love, and this couldn't be more evident than at the Portland Puppet Museum. I'm also on board with any museum that is located within a 150-year-old house. Whether that sounds terrifying or magical, you're going to want to visit. Steven Overton created this museum to share his collection of more than 2,000 puppets and his 50-plus years of experience designing and curating. Steve was a certified master puppeteer at age 22, and if you didn't know a person could get certified in such a thing, well now you do. And Steve has never stopped collecting or building. We're talking about all the species of puppets here: rod, string, hand, and shadow puppets, to name a few.

The downstairs is dedicated to all the puppets and exhibits. There are far too many, and space is far too limited, to display them all at once, so the collection necessarily rotates. There are also occasional themes and new additions that show up all the time. So even if you've already been there, you'll want to visit again. I'd like to visit more often but my daughter has

PORTLAND PUPPET MUSEUM

What: Museum and puppet theater

Where: 3906 SE Umatilla St.

Cost: Entrance is free but leave a donation.

Pro Tip: The pandemic packed a punch (if not a Judy) so donate generously.

Photo courtesy of the Portland Puppet Museum

pupaphobia (fear of puppets), and my wife won't venture near any place that might have a clown (coulrophobia).

Upstairs is the gift shop. Here you will find puppets available to purchase from all over the world, including ones the owners have built themselves. You can also purchase exquisite dollhouses, antique clocks, and build-it-yourself puppet kits.

You want to see a puppet show? That happens out back.

They just received a rare water puppet from Vietnam that I haven't seen, but don't you want to know what that is? I sure do.

ROYAL ROSARIANS MILK CARTON RACES

In the event of emergency, can my milk carton be used as a flotation device?

Portland has been hosting a Rose Festival for over a hundred years. Its big draw is the Rose Festival Parade, but parades have bored me ever since I was old enough to buy my own candy and plastic necklaces. The two boat races are the best things about the Rose Festival. I mention the Dragon Boat Race elsewhere but this entry is dedicated to the second race, a.k.a the Royal Rosarians Milk Carton Race. The event has been floating strong since 1973 and is the most Portland thing about the festival. Children and adults combine creativity, physics, athletic prowess, and dairy containers to compete for the coveted nine trophies and ribbons. Boats can be a maximum of eight feet long. The only "power" allowed is the human kind, so no

LACTOSE TOLERANT BOAT RACE

What: DIY milk jug boat races

Where: Westmoreland Park Casting Pond

Cost: Free to watch and enter

Pro Tip: A one gallon jug will float eight pounds, so math it all out carefully or you'll be drinking pond water.

If someone tries to get sneaky with styrofoam or inner tubes, or by shellacking the hull with some space-age polymer, that person will be sent home with shame upon the family.

The calcium from all that milk has made these children more buoyant.

motors. The only flotation materials allowed are milk cartons or plastic jugs.

Anything above the waterline, however is fair play, and this is where the most coveted prize comes in: The Showboat Milk Can Trophy, which is awarded for creativity. There are four racing categories: Children (ages 7-12), Adults (13 and up), Family/Multi-rider (ages 7 and up), and Corporate (Business, non-profits and loosely affiliated groups). Now, what if you don't drink milk? Portland is chock full of vegans you know, and lactose intolerance seems to be growing with every other intolerance lately. Have no fear, because local dairy Alpenrose will provide up to 50 free jugs or cartons to all participants.

If you have any questions, the person to help you is the incredibly appropriately named Connie Shipley at milkcartonboatrace@royalrosarians.com.

PORTLAND HAS TOO MANY NICKNAMES

What do locals call Portland?

Unlike San Francisco, which doesn't like to be called Frisco, or New Orleans which isn't fond of the Big Easy, Portland doesn't care what you call it. We're all about freedom of choice around here, and as a result, all the aliases stick and never die. The favorite these days seems to be Rip City. As discussed elsewhere, I'm not really a sports guy. I'm more of a *Twilight Zone* marathon kind of guy. But I'm going to tell you a basketball story: It was February 18, 1971, and the Portland Trail Blazers were playing in their first season against the LA Lakers. Blazers guard Jim Barnett launched an impossible long shot that managed to sink, and announcer Bill Schonely, overcome with emotion, screamed, "Rip city, baby!" He'd never said "rip city" before. No one had; it just wasn't a thing people said. And Schonely can't explain it either. It just came out of him—which is so goofy and wonderful that it makes it my favorite nickname for Portland, by far.

My second favorite is City of Roses, because it is also ridiculous. Most of Portland's nicknames make sense and you don't need my help. PDX—airport code. Stumptown—lots of trees=lots of stumps when the city was first getting started. Bridgetown—lots of bridges. Beervana—lots of beer. But what's

---

The only nickname that seems to have completely vanished is City of Churches. We used to have a lot of churches, but now we are one of the least churched big cities. We don't have all those stumps anymore either, but "Stumptown" has stuck like flypaper. Go figure.

Rip Taylor posing for my Rip City illustration

up with City of Roses? First mention of the nickname came from some Episcopalians here for a convention. In it, there was apparently this group of ladies who loved roses a whole lot and formed the Portland Rose Society. The next year, in advance of the 1905 Lewis and Clark Centennial Exposition, this group went nuts and planted 20 miles of our streets with roses, so visitors were misled into thinking we had an intense relationship with roses. There are other stories, but this is the one most historians believe, so I'm sticking with it.

PORTLAND'S FAKE NAMES

What: Portland's many aliases

Where: On bumper stickers and lips everywhere

Cost: Free to use—no copyright in place

Pro Tip: Go ahead and make up your own nickname for Portland. It will probably stick around. They all do.

Honorable mention goes to Little Beirut, which you hardly hear anymore, but it's an honorable name. George H. Bush called it that because of all the protesters he encountered here. You also hear P-town sometimes, but that's just laziness, I think.

THE FREAKYBUTTRUE PECULIARIUM

Where can you get your picture taken with Krampus in July and buy some bugs to snack on?

"Famed and yet unknown Portland adventurer Conrad Talmadge Elwood had a dream, but forgot it when he woke up. Still he spent a lifetime traveling the globe in search of the inexplicable and the freaky. Established in 1967, the Freakybuttrue Peculiarium is a one-of-a-kind art gallery begrudgingly devoted to Elwood's blurry vision." That's the official description.

The love child of Lisa Freeman, Mike Wellins, Colin Batty, and some rotating artists, the Peculiarium is a tribute to cryptozoology, alien abduction, and interactive mixed-media art projects. There's an alien autopsy table, a year-round Krampus (go ahead and sit in his lap and tell him what you want for Groundhog Day), a coffin to lie down in (before your number is up), a theremin to play with . . . you get the idea. A little bit of everything you want but never expected. I

THE FREAKYBUTTRUE PECULIARIUM

What: Museum of freaky and peculiar things that are 100 percent true

Where: 2234 NW Thurman St.

Cost: $5

Pro Tip: I brought my kids when they were young, but if a bathtub full of guts will upset your little ones, pay for a babysitter.

In Conrad Elwood's words, the Peculiarium is a store dedicated to learning and terror.

This dummy refused his right to an attorney.

don't want to spoil too many of the surprises here. This is not a slick place to lure tourists and cash in on Portland's "weirdness." This place is authentic (while also being full of junk, of course). Decent costumes and pets get in free. It is Portland, you know.

LINCOLN STREET KAYAK AND CANOE MUSEUM

Where can you see over 65 historically accurate kayaks and canoes?

What's the difference between a kayak and a canoe? Something to do with how you sit in it, right? I don't know much about boats, but I know someone who does. Harvey Golden. He is the answer guy for anything related to historic arctic hunting kayaks. What I love is that Harvey didn't grow up with stuff—he was driven by curiosity. In the mid-'90s, he could barely swim and had never been in a kayak before. But he wanted to. And he didn't have the money to buy one, so he decided to build one. And that led to research. And that research led him to the understanding that there are scads of different sizes and shapes of kayaks, with various strengths and weaknesses. He received the calling and became determined to build one of every kind that there ever was. He traveled around the globe to learn and document different models.

LINCOLN STREET KAYAK AND CANOE MUSEUM

What: Museum dedicated to trying to stay afloat

Where: 5340 SE Lincoln St.

Cost: Email Harvey at harveydgolden@gmail.com to arrange a visit and see if he's charging anything for a look around these days.

Pro Tip: All these boats actually function and most have been in the water. That would be the Columbia River, which is a pretty serious testing ground—er, testing water.

Ultimately Harvey ended up in what used to be a salon. It's a real "curlers to canoe" story.

Photo courtesy of the Lincoln Street Kayak and Canoe Museum

Of course, you have to put all those boats somewhere. After filling his house, then his garage, he had no choice but to open up his own museum. These things are nearly 20 feet long, after all.

BENSON BUBBLERS

What's with those rather beautiful, bronze, continuously flowing, four-headed drinking fountains you see around town?

People around here refer to drinking fountains as "bubblers." They also refer to elevators as "lifts," trunks as "boots," and chairs as "sit things." I may or may not have made some of that up. But these iconic bronze beauties are known as Benson Bubblers or just bubblers if you're feeling sleepy. They constantly bubble water so your finger doesn't get tired holding a button. And they feature four bowls, or stations, so that fistfights don't break out when somebody hogs the water fountain like at your elementary school. They're named for Simon Benson who donated 10 grand to the city in 1912 for the purpose of building and installing these bubblers. The designer was Portland architect A. E. Doyle, but "Doyle Bubblers" doesn't have the same alliterative pop, so credit goes to the guy with the checkbook. Legend has it that Benson rolled out the dough for two reasons. The first was that he was tired of loggers getting drunk on their lunch breaks. He assumed that if they had access to fresh cold water, they wouldn't need to hit that warm bottle of whiskey in their lunch box or go find a saloon, and no one would ever get drunk again. (Benson did not understand alcoholism.) The other reason—the one I suspect he made up himself—is that he saw a little girl crying on Independence Day because she was thirsty and couldn't find a drink. In

BENSON BUBBLERS

What: Not your average drinking fountains

Where: All around the city but visit the one on SW 1st and Burnside. It's the best. Not really. They're all the same.

Cost: Free!

Pro Tip: Really, go to the one at SW 1st and Burnside. It is the best.

addition to the original 20 bubblers around town, there are also some reproductions to be found. AND—there is an homage to the bubblers for doggies. Photographer William Wegman (the guy who snaps Weimaraner dogs in clothes) was paid to design a bronze dog bowl fountain on a checkerboard floor in the North Park Blocks.

Benson Bubblers pump out 100,000 gallons a day, every day of the year, unless the Portland Water Bureau decides to shut them off during a drought.

ADULT SOAP BOX DERBY

Where can you careen down an urban volcano to possible death or glory in a gravity-fueled contraption you made in your garage?

You can keep your NASCAR, Indy 500, and—well, those are the only two car races I know. But you can keep 'em! Because Portland has the best race since *Cannonball Run II* came out with Jim Nabors and Sammy Davis Jr.

Started in 1997 by Paul Zenk and Eric Foren when it was fueled by beer and a spirit of adventure, the Portland Adult Soap Box Derby has grown into a very Portland tradition, now fueled by volunteers and thrill seekers. Forty-two handmade gravity cars meet for mortal combat on the Mount Tabor track every summer. A team is four people: you must have at least three wheels, brakes, and a horn. No on-purpose suicide machines will be allowed to compete. Beyond that, competitors are encouraged to go where the gods of creativity, physics, and recklessness take them. Trophies are awarded at a party afterwards for speed, engineering, fan favorites, and the occasional lifetime achievement.

ADULT SOAP BOX DERBY

What: A very Portland sporting event

Where: Mt. Tabor Park

Cost: Free

Pro Tip: It is estimated that the event has drawn 10,000 people. Who counts them? Well, it has been speculated that estimates are based on waste volume measured by the porta-potty people. Anyone using a porta-potty in late summer is taking a bigger chance than the racers, if you ask me.

Photos courtesy of Jason DeSomer

Some favorite racers from past derbies have included a set of rotting teeth, a log car, a giant pencil, a soap on a rope, a bar on wheels (complete with tapped kegs), the Simpson family sofa, a piece of Pride cake, and the Flat Earth Research Team.

A FIVE-VOLCANO DAY

Where can you see five sleeping (but ready to wake and kill you) volcanoes within the city?

I lived here for years before anyone told me that there was a place where you could see five volcanoes at once. Then, one day at Council Crest Park, thought to be Portland's highest point at 1,073 feet above sea level, there they were: Mount Hood to the east, Mount Saint Helens and Mount Rainier to the north, Mount Adams to the northeast, and Mount Jefferson to the south. Having zero sense of direction and a third-grade grasp of geography, I had to be told by a friendly motorcyclist what I was staring at. "Oh yeah!" she said, seeing by my excitement that I was a noob. "We call this a five-volcano day. You can see them up on Rocky Butte too."

A FIVE-VOLCANO DAY

What: The best spot to try and catch them all

Where: Council Crest Park (on a clear day)

Cost: Free

Pro Tip: Parking is limited at the top, so if your lungs can take it, park at the bottom and walk (and leave the parking spot for me).

Rocky Butte, besides being a really funny name, is an extinct volcano cinder cone in the city. Portland is really laid back about volcanoes. All the guidebooks talk about Mount Hood, of course, because you can't miss it and people with money like to ski, I'm told. But what is seldom mentioned is that it is an active volcano, long overdue for a temper tantrum. And you'll hear about Mount Tabor because it's in a really cool neighborhood and there are a lot of great events in the park there. But the fact that it's a volcano? Meh. It's almost certainly dead, so who cares if you're having a picnic lunch at the lava hole? (I do!) And there are more: Powell Butte, East Butte, Mount Scott, Mount Sylvania, and Larch Mountain are extinct volcanoes just a tad outside the city itself. I spoke

Vintage postcard showing three of the five volcanoes

with a geologist who explained that "extinct" in this sense meant that it hadn't blown up in so many years that it is considered "extremely unlikely" to blow again. "Extremely unlikely," I'd like to offer the court, means kind of possible.

> Another thing that happens sometimes in Portland is a Mount Hood shadow effect, in which the mountain casts its shadow upon the sky. It looks like an upside down mountain on top of the actual mountain, making some think that Mount Hood is blowing its top—which it's totally going to do one day soon.

THE SIMPSONS TOUR

Where can you go to pay homage to the greatest cultural contribution to society from Portland (or any other American city for that matter)?

Matt Groening, the genius creator of *The Simpsons*, grew up on Evergreen Terrace, just like Bart, Lisa, Maggie, and Santa's Little Helper. That street's name is just one homage to his hometown. I'm sure this is an incomplete list, but here are the *Simpsons*-related sites that I have been able to dig up:

First, Lincoln High School. Groening, like Mel Blanc (discussed elsewhere in these pages) graduated from Lincoln High. What are the odds that two such prominent legends in animation went to the same high school? I looked it up and you'd have better chances finding a dry month in a Portland winter. But it happened! And Groening gifted the blessed ground by drawing Bart in the cement along with his signature and "Class of 1972."

Montgomery Park and Burnside Street were mashed together to name Charles Montgomery Burns, filthy-rich owner of the nuclear plant and brittle bones.

Bart's best friend is Milhouse Van Houten, and we do have a Van Houten Avenue here. Groening hasn't owned up to borrowing the name, but my theory is that he was thinking of Charlie Brown's best friend, Linus Van Pelt, and that blended with Van Houten Avenue in his subconscious.

You can raise a pint at the Lucky Labrador on Northwest Quimby Street to Springfield mayor Diamond Joe Quimby.

Groening tells the story of his friend who used to think his prayers went to the giant illuminated sign on top of what was then the Montgomery Ward building.

Montgomery Park, inspiration for Mr. Montgomery Burns

Then hop a Portland Streetcar on Lovejoy Street in honor of Reverend Lovejoy who loves trains. Raise a cone at Salt and Straw on Kearney Street to Springfield Elementary's nineteen-year-old fifth grader Kearney Zzyzwicz and his teenage son.

Ned Flanders was named after Flanders Street and you should visit the northeast side because someone has undoubtedly added a *D* to spell out *NED*, and if they haven't, it's your obligation to get the job done.

THE REAL SPRINGFIELD IS IN OREGON

What: *The Simpsons* landmarks

Where: All over town

Cost: Free

Pro Tip: Groening lived at 742 SW Evergreen Terrace, but don't knock on the door or the current occupants will "have a cow, man," and tell you to "eat their shorts."

And finally, my favorite is Terwilliger Boulevard. It is the namesake of Sideshow Bob Terwilliger, of course. And like Bob, Terwilliger is dangerous and twisted like Bob's hair and devious mind. Stop at historic Pronto Pup, because Pronto Pups were actually served at sideshows for decades.

REMEMBERING VANPORT

What happened to Oregon's second-largest largest city?

Vanport was eliminated in a single day: Memorial Day 1948. Vanport's name derived from its halfway point between the cities of Portland and Vancouver in the Columbia River flood plain. It was only around for about six years but profoundly changed Portland in ways that are still observable today.

World War II led to an employment boom around Portland, including in the three ship factories of Edgar Kaiser. But when workers rolled in, there were limited housing opportunities, especially for Black families who weren't allowed to own property inside Portland. Kaiser wanted to hold on to his skilled workers, so he talked the federal government into paying for a massive housing project that would be located centrally to his three factories. It was its own city consisting of just under 10,000 apartments, mostly crammed into 14-unit segregated buildings with paper-thin walls and painted gray. Vanport had a movie theater, school, hospital, and day care center.

THE SPIRIT OF VANPORT

What: A memorial to the lost town of Vanport

Where: 1810 SW 5th Ave.

Cost: Free

Pro Tip: Visit vanportmosaic.org to learn much more and donate to the cause.

I'll have to skip over some important history here and hit the bullet points; Vanport Black families organized a tenant's league, which fought the housing authority's Jim Crow schemes and rallied for nonracist employment policies. They held demonstrations, called in the NAACP and the new Urban League of Portland, and won some battles.

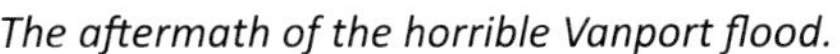

The aftermath of the horrible Vanport flood.

The war ended, the ship jobs with it, and most of those who were able, left. Now, Vanport was primarily populated by Black families, since the cards were stacked against them. Civic leaders plotted to demolish it and reclaim the land. Then, after weeks of heavy rain, the river crested 15 feet higher than the flood plain. Vanport sat low and was protected by "dikes" that turned out to be just a railroad berm. Officials told the citizens all was fine, but in the end, the soil mound wasn't enough to keep back the water and the sirens blared—giving all 18,500 inhabitants just 35 minutes to escape via the one uphill road. The government listed 15 dead, but the number was higher. The flood easily took out the cheap housing and washed away cars, leaving nearly all residents homeless and without transportation.

Now refugees, they flooded into Portland. But they brought with them all they had learned about organizing and protests. They formed the Vanport Citizens' Emergency Disaster Committee and fought for compensation, recognition, and decent housing. They formed a caravan to the state capital and staged marches. The only upshot of this horror story is that the organizing and protesting interspersed among the victories of the civil rights era and were passed to the next generation to continue the fight.

Part of the fight is remembering Vanport so it won't be repeated. To that end, the Vanport Mosaic exists. They are a "museum without walls" and bring in exhibits, tours, festivals, art, and theater.

One permanent memorial the Vanport Mosaic created is an exhibit at the entrance to the new Vanport Building of Portland State University. It features a mural by Portland artist Alex Chiu titled *The Spirit of Vanport.*

THE CAPTAIN'S WHEEL AT DAN AND LOUIS OYSTER BAR

Where can you dine on bivalves and view a treasure reclaimed from an 1865 shipwreck?

The SS *Brother Jonathan* was a side-wheeler steamship that sailed from San Francisco in July 1865, headed for Portland. It never made it past Crescent City. The ship was overloaded, it seems, with cargo that included a chest of gold, rare coins, and the belongings of its 223 passengers. A storm caused the side-wheeler to hit the Saint George Reef with such force that anyone on deck got tossed right into the ocean. Forty-five minutes later, the ship was at the bottom of the ocean, leaving only 19 survivors.

For more than a century, legends were tossed about concerning the location of the SS *Brother Jonathan* and what treasures might be reclaimed. In 1993, most questions were answered when the wreckage was discovered by a team of scientists and historians. Many valuable coins were found. But to me, the real treasure was the reclaimed captain's wheel. It now rests in the front lobby at the Dan and Louis Oyster Bar, ultimately making it to its intended destination of Portland but not in the manner expected.

Brother Jonathan was an early mascot for America, like Uncle Sam, which explains the steamer's name. This was also the ship that brought Oregon the message that it had gained statehood.

The Brother Jonathan

The Dan and Louis Oyster Bar is itself a historic landmark. It's been here for over a century, founded in 1919, and continues to be renowned for its piping-hot oyster stew. The restaurant is still run by the Wachsmuth family (now in its fifth generation at the shell game).

BIVALVES AND THE *BROTHER JONATHAN*

What: The SS *Brother Jonathan*'s captain's wheel

Where: Dan and Louis Oyster Bar, 208 SW Ankeny St.

Cost: A cup of that historic oyster stew will only set you back $8.

Pro Tip: The myth that oysters should only be eaten in months with an *R* doesn't hold water here. The pristine and frigid waters of Yaquina Bay keep them tasty all year.

PORTLAND STREET ART ALLIANCE

You can't miss bumping into some world-class murals here, but how in the world do you find the best street art on purpose?

Portland has too many one-way streets to make mural appreciation an easy thing. Most of the time you're tooling down the road, dodging pedestrians, bicyclists, other cars, and bus lanes, trying to read tiny, bent street signs that have been rendered illegible by the rain—and that's when you glimpse some masterpiece in your peripheral. There's no place to pull over. You think maybe you'll go around the block and find a parking spot, but you can't make a turn for 17 intersections. This is one of the many reasons the Portland Street Art Alliance is an art lover's best buddy.

PORTLAND MURALS

What: Some of the finest street art in the world

Where: In every part of the city

Cost: Free

Pro Tip: To see a lot of great murals in one short stretch, take a stroll down Alberta Street.

I don't have space to do them justice here, but here's a brief encapsulation of PSAA: a nonprofit organization and network of artists, academics, and art pros who help facilitate city art projects, document them, educate the public, provide platforms for networking, organize events, restore artwork, and promote progressive urban policies concerning our artistic community. If you live here, are an artist, or care about supporting the arts, all of those things I listed are reasons you should go to pdxstreetart.org and see what they're up to and how you can help (or partner up, or access their services).

One of our many stunning murals

But for our purposes here, let's focus on that education bit. PSAA offers tours of some of Portland's best street art. Not only will PSAA directors take you by the hand and show you the good stuff, but they will give you the lowdown on Portland's rich history of graffiti art and murals, tell you about the projects happening now, and perhaps change the way you think about public space. This is a walking tour, but private tours are easily arranged. All proceeds go to a noble cause so you can feel good about that, too.

Don't have time for a tour? PSAA has your back. Their website offers beautifully designed walking and biking maps that are free to download. Street art, by its nature, comes and goes, but they strive to keep us current and informed. Be sure to download the latest maps if you plan to chart your own street art tour.

THE PORTLAND PODIUMS

Where is there a great place to air your grievances, announce your bid for mayor, or warn others of impending doom?

There's nothing to prevent you from making a speech in any public spot in the city, of course, but Portland does have a designated spot for it. The MAX Blue Line stops in the Goose Hollow neighborhood right by Providence Park stadium, which is why it's called Providence Park Station (I figured that out all by myself). And there you will find bronze podiums, which were put there by the city to "invite spontaneous oratory." Yes, you can get on up there and make a speech any time you want, and yes, people sometimes do exactly that—particularly after many beers have been had after a soccer match at the nearby stadium.

THE PORTLAND PODIUMS

What: Functional art

Where: Providence Park MAX Station

Cost: Free (like your speech)

Pro Tip: There are local laws against handing out bills, shouting profanity, and threatening people, so how freely you can speak without Johnny Law doing something about it is questionable.

In 1998, when the westside design team of artists were tasked with providing some public art at the station, the stadium

---

A tree stump, a Greek column, and (my favorite) a wooden box now await MAX passengers—a tribute to orators past and in anticipation of those to come.

Podiums at Goose Hollow, courtesy of TriMet

still went by the name Civic Stadium. Side note on that: the stadium has existed since 1893 in one form or another and has been known by various monikers, all of which make it the oldest soccer stadium in the country. Anyhoo, the artists were invited to play with the "civic" theme, so the plaza became an homage to the importance of oratory to Portland's civic history.

SQUATCHIN' IT UP

Where can you lay your eyes on some actual Bigfoot evidence and artifacts?

Technically, this place is located a half hour outside Portland, but do you want to see Bigfoot or not? And you'll be going to Boring, Oregon, so you can take a picture of the town sign while you're there (also mentioned are Boring's sister cities: Dull, Scotland, and Bland, Australia). Why is it in Boring? Because the area surrounding Mount Hood has the most reported Bigfoot sightings in the whole state.

The North American Bigfoot Center is staffed with Bigfoot experts to answer any and all questions you might want to throw at them. Technically, these people are known as sasquatchologists, although when I visited, people seemed to think I made that word up and were certainly annoyed with the way I worked it into the hundreds of questions I posed. Seriously, though, these people know their Bigfoot. The NABC is the brainchild of Cliff Barackman, whom Bigfoot aficionados will know from Animal Planet's *Finding Bigfoot*. For nearly three decades, Cliff has been researching Bigfoot, and he is considered a top expert in the field. Bobcat Goldthwait, by the way, who directed the best Bigfoot movie of all time, *Willow Creek*, is a friend of Cliff and his wife and undoubtedly tapped their deep knowledge for the film.

NORTH AMERICAN BIGFOOT CENTER

What: Bigfoot museum

Where: 31297 SE Hwy. 26

Cost: $8 general admission, $6 for kids, vets, seniors, etc.

Pro Tip: Hard to find (like Bigfoot!). Just look for the "Ashley's" sign at the intersection of Hwy 26 and Hwy 212, and they are right there next to the pizza place, the Chevron station, and Chester's Pub.

Left: *Sign coming into Boring*
Right: *Murphy, courtesy of Northwest Bigfoot Museum*

What kinds of treasures lie within? They recently put a Bigfoot nest on display, for starters. And there are foot casts galore for you to get up close and personal with. You want to know what a Bigfoot smells like? They've got something for you to sniff. Educational displays abound, and there is even the Boggy Creek Theater on site that shows various Bigfoot documentaries.

The star of the show is "Murphy," their life-sized Sasquatch replica that you will want to use as a backdrop for next year's holiday photo.

PAUL BONEYAN VS. PAUL BUNYAN

Where can you visit both a Paul Bunyan AND a Paul Boneyan statue in the same day?

Okay, let's start with the traditional Paul Bunyan first. If you love roadside attractions, this is a great one. Paul has been standing over the Kenton area of Portland since 1959, when he was put there to commemorate the 100th year of Oregon being a state. Kenton had a big Centennial Expo, and what says Stumptown better than a bearded giant with a huge axe to make stumps with? He stands 31 feet tall and is made out of concrete and steel, just like the real Paul Bunyan.

Paul BONEyan, on the other hand, is made of bone. Plastic bone. He hovers over a northeast neighborhood at the corner of Northeast Rodney Avenue and Northeast Holman Street. Clocking it at a slightly less impressive 12 feet, he greets the neighborhood all year long, donning lights and a hat for the current holiday season. There's a plaque on the fence that is worth your time to read.

Paul is far from being the only skinless person on the streets. I haven't been able to pin down the origins, but all over the city I've found skeletons hanging around, doing odd things. Most of them are sitting on bicycles or hanging on a fence. I was at the Pix-O-Matic last week and there are some skeletons break-dancing on cardboard out back for no apparent reason.

So, Bone or Bun—who is best in the Northwest? Bun is taller and listed on the National Register of Historic Places. But Bone has a better plaque and has that Portland DIY vibe. I'm afraid it's a draw.

Paul Bunyan and Paul Boneyan

My favorite sits on one of those tall bikes in front of a bicycle shop on Multnomah Boulevard. He changes his outfit often and generally seems to be in a good mood most of the time. I call him the Bone Ranger, but that almost certainly is not the name he was given at birth. Why all the skeletons? Who started this trend? I want to know, but I also don't want to know, you know? And in the end, there probably isn't a real answer to be had. It's like garden gnomes and pink flamingos—just catches on like chicken pox.

BONE OR BUN?

What: Dueling giants

Where: Boneyan is situated in northeast Portland and Bunyan is at the southwest corner of N Denver Ave. and N Interstate Ave.

Cost: Free

Pro Tip: Join the Facebook page Hidden Portland for regular skeletal spotting.

AND SPEAKING OF SKELETONS

Where could I go in Portland to find a human skull or maybe a bat skeleton? Mother's Day is coming up . . .

The best place for bones is a place called Paxton Gate, located in the Mississippi district. Here, you can find various taxidermy, skulls and skeletons, jars of preserved baby animals, and insects with giant mandibles, just to name a few.

Of course, this is Portland, so no animals were actually harmed for the purpose of sale. They assure you everything is ethically sourced, so you can buy that skull without worrying about putting money in a poacher's pocket.

Another place for curiosities of this sort is the Skeleton Key Vintage. I find it witchier here with less of a Museum of Natural History vibe. This is the place I'd go if I needed a really creepy antique baby doll or a pentagram throw rug. There was also a vintage saxophone when I was there last, so I shouldn't try to put them in any box. This is Portland, after all.

PAXTON GATE AND SKELETON KEY

What: Oddities shops

Where: 4204 N Mississippi Ave. and 3352 SE Belmont St.

Cost: Depends on whether you're buying a skull or the whole skeleton

Pro Tip: Talk to the staff. They love what they do and have good stories about whatever you're looking at.

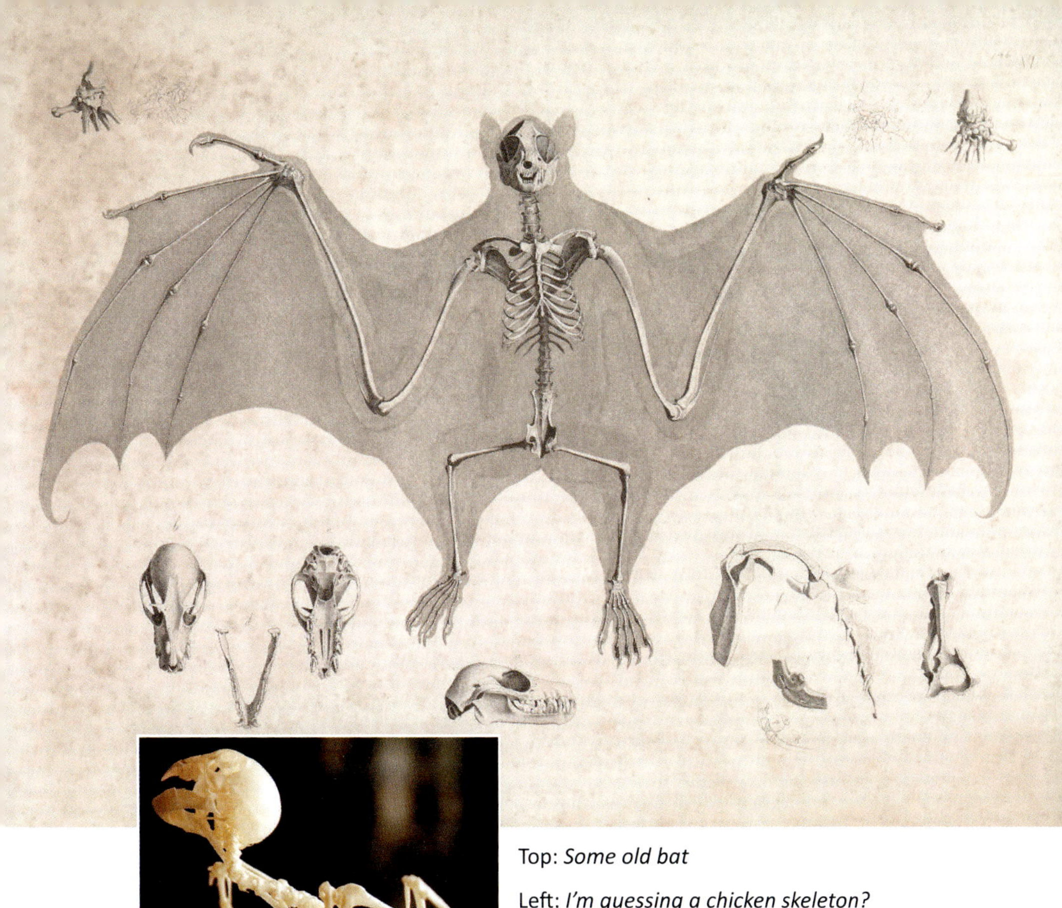

Top: *Some old bat*

Left: *I'm guessing a chicken skeleton?*

Portland is home to the Portland Oddities and Curiosities Expo that comes around every year, complete with sideshow performances and plenty of jewelry made from bugs and bones.

SIGNS OF THE TIMES

Where does art meet science, typography, history, capitalism, and nostalgia?

There are many reasons to love true neon lighting. For me, it's akin to my love for vinyl records and pinball machines. The march of technology left them in the dust, but they offer ineffable qualities. Then there is the science of neon. We're looking at electrified gas sealed in tubes and the choice of gas determines the color. Neon itself gives off a gorgeous orange. Mercury gives you blue. Helium gives yellow. The artistic shaping of the glass tubes into a form of advertising first showed up at a Packard dealership in LA. By the '30s, neon lighting was popping up across the country. Most evidence of that first decade of neon signage has been wiped out, but Portland has magnificent examples that go back to the '40s. Obviously the Portland Stag sign gets all the love and postcards, but many other pieces of historic signage light up neighborhoods in every pocket of the city.

Perhaps second in popularity to the Stag is the Palms Motor Hotel sign, an impressive 50-foot specimen on North Interstate Avenue that dates to possibly 1952. People from around the globe stop to take their pictures in front of it. Featuring a giant palm tree, a coconut-throwing monkey, and a pink-light offer of free TV, it is a kitsch classic. The Portland Outdoor sign is another favorite, lurching three stories up: a blue-clad cowboy bucks around on a perfectly orange neon horse above brilliant pink letters.

Grill on Southeast 82nd, with its rare example of Chinese restaurant neon signage, has been around since 1944.

Courtesy of Jason Moore

The Water Heater King is a Portland legend, lighting up Foster Road and selling plumbing supplies since 1946. The recently renovated Capitol Hill Motel houses one of my favorite neon signs (on Barbur Boulevard) and, of course, the Bagdad Theater sign is just amazing.

Portland is too rich in this endangered art form for me to discuss them all. Luckily, we have a local resource to help us—Kate Widdows, an independent letterer and typographer and expert in all things neon. Kate will tell you that neon is one art form that does not translate to photography or video. You have to see it with your own eyes—watch the gas swirling inside the tubes and the different luminosity that comes from different gases. She has mapped these treasures for us, and the chart is available on her website: katewiddows.com.

NEON WONDERLAND

What: Vintage neon art

Where: All over town

Cost: Free

Pro Tip: Go see the sign at Chin's in the Hollywood District because they also have handmade dumplings.

HIDDEN TEA WIZARDS

Where can you sip Chinese tea sourced from sacred places and vibrationally charged by a wizard–and get a tarot reading?

Fly Awake is truly a secret place. And by that, I mean it's actually hidden down an alley behind an adult novelty store. Portland!

Okay, first, let's talk about tea. We're talking full Chinese tea service with the finest teas sourced from magical places. The purple beauty, for instance, is "sourced from the purple leaves of the deep-rooted old trees on Jongmai Mountain." The golden water turtle is sourced from the Wu Yi mountain region and its description claims: "Drink this punch like a well defended Hero, and like some kind of miracle, puppet strings will grow from your fingertips. Use your Will wisely!" Yeah, this isn't your old lady's tea shop.

Fly Awake is also known for their tea subscriptions. Each month the tea wizards congregate and choose three small-batch teas to send out into the world for $35.

And speaking of those wizards? You'll find them there in the shop, ready to raise the vibration of your tea and to read your tarot cards for you. A basic tarot card reading is just $20, by the way. Not a bad price to see into the future. You will generally find a tarot reading tea wizard on site, but appointments are available by calling them at (503) 867-8905. You can also hire

FLY AWAKE TEA HOUSE

What: Tea shop and tarot readings

Where: 909 N Beech St., off N Mississippi and behind SheBop

Cost: Service for one is in the neighborhood of $8 and a guru's chai will run you $5.

Pro Tip: They also sell tea online, and I suggest you buy "drunken concubine" because that's one great name.

A cup of magical tea, courtesy of Fly Awake Tea House

the tea wizards to come to your party and provide the whole expert tea service experience. They do weddings, dinners, or just friendly hangouts. Would you like them to add some tarot card reading to that tea? No problem!

> They offer special events and classes as well. On tea? Yes, but also about dreaming and herbs and tarot—oh my!

UNDERGROUND DRINKING

Where can you do some subterranean imbibing like in the speakeasy days?

Legally, we don't have to hide our gin and tonics by drinking in basements anymore, but it's fun to pretend. Portland has several options for that '20s vibe. I'll mention a few here:

Bible Club: "Praise the Lord and pass the booze!" is the motto here, and this gin joint is full-on Great Gatsby: antique barstools, copper ceiling, and old-timey photos on the wall. Designed like an actual Prohibition-style speakeasy, Bible Club is truly like stepping back in time. You'll be surrounded by delicate antiques from the era, sultry jazz music, and creative libations that are a strong nod to the cocktails of the past.

Les Caves: If you're looking for less make-believe and more wine cave, Les Caves has to be the coziest place to have a bottle below ground. Les Caves is on the intimate side. It's laid back, not stuffy or snobby like some other wine bars that intimidate me. There's a hideaway nook with a sofa—so a tucked-away place inside a tucked-away place, which makes it the most tucked-away public space where you can have a glass of wine in the city.

Mummy's: is the place to go if you want to feel like you're in an Indiana Jones movie. This bar has been around since 1980,

SUBTERRANEAN COCKTAILS

What: Literal underground bars

Where: Bible Club, 6716 SE 16th Ave.; Les Caves, 1719 Alberta St.; Mummy's, 622 SW Columbia St.; Ash Bar, 575 NE 24th Ave.; The Eastburn, 1800 E Burnside St.

Cost: Varies

Pro Tip: The Whiskey Library has the speakeasy vibe, but because it's upstairs it didn't make my list. But check it out if whiskey is your thing.

which almost makes it an antiquity in this city. You'll descend to a world of hieroglyphics and sarcophagi to order your baba ghanoush and a Pyramid Brewing pale ale to wash it down. You get the idea. My favorite part is the funerary figure named IY, carved by the owner and placed in the middle of the bar as an homage to his birthplace in Egypt.

Ash Bar: is hidden under Nomad, which is a swanky restaurant that people go to on their honeymoon. This is the place to go if you like some windows in your subterranean drinking establishments—and some uptown cocktails with exotic ingredients I can't pronounce. But don't worry about Ash being too sophisticated for a good time. Go online to see the profane name for their fish sandwich and it should put you at ease.

The Eastburn: If you're looking for less of a speakeasy vibe and more of a retro basement party, you can go downstairs at Eastburn. They have a great selection of high-quality local beers and ciders, a couple of big screens, exotic fish tanks, a dance floor, a Pac Man Battle Royale table, and—most importantly—two Skee-Ball lanes.

The Pope House: Pope House Bourbon Lounge has a speakeasy-like lower level that specializes in experimental cocktails and spins records on a turntable.

If the Bible Club sounds too swanky for you, they offer the Revival Backyard Patio, which is a much more casual affair where you can have a beer and bring your dog.

THE MYSTERIOUS PORTLAND WEATHER MACHINE

What if you'd like to know the day's weather but you'd like it in the most interesting way possible?

Of course, if you want to know what the rest of the day has in store for you weather-wise, you could look at your cell phone. But that's not the Portland way. Go be boring somewhere else. What you want to do is go downtown to Portland's Pioneer Courthouse Square just before noon. Head over to the bricks below Starbucks and wait by that 30-foot column with the sphere at the top. Why? Because at noon, you will hear a fanfare of trumpets! Lights flash! A foggy mist sprays from above, obscuring the entrance of the creature who will eventually emerge from that sphere and predict what the day has in store for the next 24 hours. Will it be a mist-blowing dragon, which portends scary weather? The blue heron for drizzle? Or the sun for a sunny day?

Two wind scoops forged of bronze spin below the stainless steel orb if the wind is acting up. There are a series of lights along the side that tell the temperature, but you've got to know the system: Red lights indicate every ten degrees. Blue lights are for degrees below freezing and white bulbs herald above-

---

The inspiration for the weather machine goes to Will Martin, the Portland-ish architect who designed Pioneer Square and made a place for a future weather machine, complete with outlandish sketches of his own visions of what it could be.

Left: *The* Portland Weather Machine

Right: *Detail of the sun that dominates Portland's summers*

freezing weather. Up by the sphere there are lights that show air quality: green, amber, and red.

The weather machine has been standing there since 1988. Dick Ponzi was the brilliant engineer who designed the magical contraption. Jere and Ray Grimm were the artists, together with Roger Patrick Sheppard, who helped bring it to life over the span of eleven months. Luke Grimm, the artists' son, is now the wizard in charge of making sure it keeps doing its thing.

PORTLAND WEATHER MACHINE

What: Weather beacon and lumina kinetic bronze sculpture

Where: Pioneer Courthouse Square

Cost: Free

Pro Tip: The fanfare you hear is the beginning of Aaron Copland's "Fanfare for the Common Man." Impress somebody with that some time.

WORLD'S TALLEST BARBER POLE

Where can you go to honor all the brave, fallen barbershop quartets?

Okay, this . . . er, landmark is about a half-hour drive from Portland, but I'm including it to annoy my wife who has a pathological fear/hatred of barbershop quartets. Forest Grove is quaint as hell, but she won't go near it because the town has a strong historical tie to barbershop music, and you never know when one of those straw-hatted, mustachioed groups is going to pop out from behind a bush.

The blame—I mean, credit—goes to a men's chorus in the mid-'40s called the Gleemen who hosted an old-timey barbershop competition. The town hadn't heard Chuck Berry yet, so they got people to attend the one-day event and it was a big hit! Soon, the one-day contest morphed into a whole weekend celebration known as the Gay '90s Festival. People came by the thousands. School children dressed in period costumes. Local shops decorated their windows like it was 1890. There was a parade and a mustache contest! By the actual '90s (the 1990s), the festival had run out of gas. But they still do that barbershop competition. And all this has earned Forest Grove the title Ballad Town USA.

WORLD'S TALLEST BARBER SHOP POLE

What: Monument to old-timey music

Where: Lincoln Park in Forest Grove

Cost: Free

Pro Tip: The original pole sported a foam ball at the top, but it has since been replaced with a fine glass one. Point that out on your next date to Lincoln Park and enjoy a well-earned smooch.

Ripley's piece featuring our barber pole

Who gave it that name? I don't know, but I'm giving it to barbershop balladeer Chuck Olson, who is also credited with the brilliant idea of a giant barbershop pole. It was the 1973 Barbershop Harmony Society convention in Portland. Chuck had once been to a convention in Texas where they had a 40-foot barbershop pole and remembered the tear it brought to many an eye. He knew he could acquire a much bigger pole here, where the trees put Texas twigs to shame. So he did. A 72-footer. And he got his barbershop buddies to help him paint it up. One assumes they sang "Hello Ma Baby" the whole time. Anyhoo, the pole now stands with honor just off the main street in Lincoln Park.

A local lumber company donated an 80-foot pole to the cause, which earned a coveted Guinness World Record certificate.

SETZIOL DOORS

Where can you lay your eyes on a rare Leroy Setziol piece?

Leroy Setziol was a former minister and it shows in his work. When he landed in Portland and came across Native American art, it was that spiritual approach that inspired him to teach himself to carve wood in 1952. His work was almost immediately appreciated by the midcentury architects of the Pacific Northwest, and he was commissioned to create panels and doors to add warmth, texture, and feeling to their minimalist structures. Setziol created more than panels and doors. He did sculptures and furniture. But because his doors faced the world and graced public places, that's the art that gets most recognized. And I suspect those large canvases are where he found the most joy. Though Setziol got the respect of architects from the jump, his reputation has only grown, and in the art world, that often means less public access. Most of his work is in private collections, closed off to most of us. You'll still pass his work now and again; one of his pieces recently appeared at a salvage place in town—dumped by someone who didn't know what they had. Occasionally an art museum will get the collectors to part with his pieces long enough to do a show. But this is rare. I know of four places you can easily see his work, however. One panel hangs at the entry foyer of Eliot

ROY SETZIOL PANELS

What: Local art legend's wood carvings

Where: Eliot Hall at Reed College, Mittleman Jewish Community Center at 6651 SW Capitol Hwy., Nordia House at 8800 SW Oleson Rd., and University of Portland at 5000 N Willamette Blvd.

Cost: Free

Pro Tip: The chapel doors are made from the salvaged wood of storm-damaged walnut trees.

Setziol Door at PSU

Hall at Reed College. Another graces the lobby at Mittleman Jewish Community Center in Multnomah Village. The third serves as the entrance door at Nordia House in the Garden Home neighborhood. The Nordia House door was a joint project between Roy and his daughter Monica Setziol-Phillips, who finished the job after her father's death. Fourth—and perhaps my favorite—are the doors at University of Portland Chapel.

> "Art is anything that is made, and an artist is a worker—like anyone else—except he deals with ideas, beliefs, and the realm of the spirit. A well-made tool is a hell of a lot more beautiful than a copied oil painting. That it is utilitarian is beside the point." —Leroy Setziol

THE OTHER INDEPENDENT BOOKSTORES

Is Powell's the only bookstore in town?

Most people already know about Powell's. Seems like everybody does, and everybody should. It's the biggest independent bookstore in the world and one of the greatest things about Portland. But we have other bookstores to try and keep afloat, and you don't always want to get lost in Powell's all day or fight the summer crowds for a parking space. It's also a different experience, poking around a cozy mom-and-pop bookstore and chatting with the book lover behind the counter. I hope these stores still have their heads up by the time you read this. The pandemic is trying its best to wipe out the last of the noble bookshops.

THE OTHER INDEPENDENTS

What: Indy bookstores

Where: Broadway Books, 1714 NE Broadway; Green Bean Books, 1600 NE Alberta St.; Mother Foucault's Bookshop, 523 SE Morrison St.; Monograph Bookwerks, 5005 NE 27th Ave.; Annie Bloom's Books, 7834 SW Capitol Hwy.

Cost: Worth it—you're saving the independent bookstore!

Pro Tip: That bookstore lampooned on *Portlandia*, In Other Words, is sadly closed.

Broadway Books had been around since 1992. It's a female-owned shop on NE Broadway (no, not the one satirized on *Portlandia*). They have a great selection, and you won't get better service anywhere. They host author events too. Green Bean Books is the place for kids' books. Tucked away in a little red house, they have a great selection, and you can buy mustaches from a vending

Mother Foucault's Bookshop

machine there. Perfection. Mother Foucault's Bookshop is our most beatnik bookstore and is reassuringly old school. Actual hardwood bookshelves tower over you, stuffed with tomes of philosophy, poetry, and fine literature. Messy desks here and there tell you that this is the real deal. They also host poetry readings and local bands. Monograph Bookwerks specializes in art books as well as actual art. Comic book shops abound (Dark Horse is stationed nearby). Bridge City Comics, Floating World Comics, and Things from Another World are just a few top shops, but there are thankfully many.

Annie Bloom's Books is one of my favorite independent bookshops, and a great reason to visit Multnomah Village, which is otherwise full of other local shops and restaurants (Thai Herbs has my favorite fried rice, FYI). Annie's has a great selection, a knowledgeable staff, and a roaming kitty cat.

NURSERY RHYME NIGHTMARE JUICE

Where can you go if you're sleeping too well and would like more waking hours to get things done?

I'm pretty sure the Enchanted Forest was created to ensure bad dreams. It's about 45 minutes outside Portland in the town of Turner, but absolutely worth it. You know how antique dolls, puppets, clowns, and twins standing by elevators are horribly frightening? This is a whole theme park like that. It was hand-built by Roger Tofte in the late '60s and took him seven years complete. He and his family have added to it since then and it now covers 20 acres out in the woods. It started with Storybook Lane, and that's really what I want to talk about. You enter through a giant witch's gaping maw. Then you walk around from one terrifying diorama to the next. Cement sculptures of fairy tale characters (think Grimm's, not Disney) greet you at every turn, along with animatronics (which are just puppets powered by gears instead of strings, right?). Little Miss Muffet will scare the daylights out of you, but Peter Pumpkin Eater is the biggest villain here, standing all smug and creepy outside his easy, imprisoned wife-in-a-pumpkin-shell. Pinocchio isn't as scary as you think he's going to be, but the Blue Fairy blasts from the wardrobe, looking like a sea hag coming to eat your soul. Alice and the hookah-smoking caterpillar on the 'shroom is scary enough, but then there's a rabbit hole, which is a claustrophobic tunnel of darkness and dread that goes on

GOOD TIMES & BAD DREAMS

What: The Enchanted Forest

Where: 8462 Enchanted Way SE, Turner

Cost: $19–$22

Pro Tip: The haunted house is an extra $4 over admission but worth it.

Left: *Entrance to Enchanted Forest*

Right: *The spider here, not nearly as terrifying as Ms. Muffet*

for about 50 feet. There's a haunted house that is truly haunting, but not as much as that rabid robot dog at the shooting gallery in Western Town (imagine Westworld). I haven't scratched the surface of this place, but go see it for yourself. It is charming and sweet and bloodcurdling. Roger Tofte himself can be seen zipping around on his scooter, as his daughter's music (she's a Paris-trained harpsichordist) tinkles all over the park. I stopped Roger once to thank him for this amazing art project he's given us and he couldn't have been humbler or sweeter—like Mr. Rogers, really, who also gave me nightmares. That Lady Elaine Fairchilde puppet? *Shudder* . . .

The 1968 Humpty Dumpty took a great fall in 2014, and all the kings horses and all the—well, you know how it goes. But it was replaced quickly to avoid patrons being shell-shocked when the park opened the following year.

A CONTEST FOR THE CHICKENHEARTED

Want to see an unscripted contest where competitors are just winging it?

As a vegetarian, this is the only hot wing contest I can truly endorse. I'm talking about the Lents Chicken Beauty Contest, held each summer. Although there is no longer a swimsuit category and the formal wear category had to be eliminated as well (making chickens wear high heels is just cruel), this is one of the few remaining beauty contests in the country that does not pretend to be anything but skin deep. There is no talent portion and the contestants make no speeches about world peace. It is acceptable to discuss breasts and legs, but frowned upon to make comments about eating them.

Whether you prefer blondes, brunettes, redheads, spangled, or mottled, this annual event will make you say, "Now *that* is a beautiful chicken." I admit that I thought I was immune to the charms of chickens myself, but

THE LENTS CHICKEN BEAUTY CONTEST

What: A beauty contest—for chickens!

Where: 9330 SE Harold St.

Cost: Free

Pro Tip: While you're in the neighborhood, drive by 6109 SE 92nd Ave. because Woody Guthrie lived and composed music there.

The event is just one part of the annual Lents neighborhood street fair. So even if you don't like pretty chickens, there will be 50-or-so craft and food vendors and an international food market.

A really good-looking chicken

one look at a Sebright or *Barbu d'Uccle* will change a fellow's mind. The last trophy went to a Tolbunt Polish hen, and if that bird with its pom-pom hairdo didn't resemble my prom date in '87 with her sky-high Aquanet-and-curling-ironed hair, I'll eat my cummerbund. But don't bring your rooster to ogle the ladies. Roosters are not allowed in Portland, which is oddly intolerant for such a progressive town, but they do make a lot of noise and no one wants to encourage underground cockfights.

DRAGON BOATS

What's the story with those beautiful boats on the river, decorated with Chinese dragon heads?

Dragon boats, as one would expect by looking at them, originated in China. They've been around for at least 2,000 years, although Dragon Boat racing didn't reach international sport status until 1976, and didn't become a Portland tradition until 1989.

Portland is lucky enough to have two big dragon boat races, both at Tom McCall Waterfront Park. One is part of the Rose Festival in June, and the other, the Portland Dragon Boat Festival, happens in September.

The Rose Festival race is hosted by the Portland–Kaohsiung Sister City Association. It features up to 96 dragon boat teams from all over the world competing in three divisions: high school, women, and mixed. The boats themselves are known as Taiwan-style and they feature the traditional colorful dragon head and tail. They seat 20 paddlers, one tiller, one caller, and one flag catcher. That flag catcher is responsible for grabbing the flag off their designated buoy, which is the signal that the boat has finished its heat.

Hundreds of people will gather at the Willamette River for the ancient Chinese Eye Dotting Ceremony. In this ceremony, red dots are painted on the eyes of the dragon boats. This officially wakes the dragons and announces the beginning of the Rose Festival Dragon Boat Race season.

DRAGON BOAT FESTIVALS

What: Boat races using traditional Chinese dragon boats

Where: Tom McCall Waterfront Park

Cost: Free to watch

Pro Tip: If you want to race one day, drop in on an open practice at DragonSports USA for just $2. Visit dragonsports.org for details.

The head of a dragon boat

There's another festival, without all the parades, that is simply called the Portland Dragon Boat Festival. Organized by DragonSports USA, this race is popular with dragon boaters around the Pacific Northwest. There is a junior division for less than hard-core boaters and a specialty division for groups like breast cancer survivors and senior groups. It takes place between the Hawthorne Bridge and RiverPlace. It's a festival, and in Portland, so there will be beer.

Festivals aside, dragon boating is getting really popular here. Now there are teams that practice year-round. DragonSports USA will set you up with a team that suits you and your schedule. There are women's teams, youth teams, age 50+ teams, breast cancer survivor teams, and mixed teams. Without paying the one-time membership fee, you can drop in and paddle with a team of your choice three times to see if you like it.

You don't have to know anything about paddling to give it a try.

NORDIA HOUSE

Where can you get a good game of Kubb in this town?

I found out about Nordia House about a month ago, when I was in search of remaining public Leroy Setziol doors (discussed elsewhere). Just goes to show you how much there is to discover here and that I will be kicking myself when I find yet another great thing the minute I turn in this manuscript to the publisher. Oh well.

Nordia House is a beautiful Nordic oasis tucked away in the hilly green of southwest Portland that celebrates all things in the Nordic past and present. For those who took the same terrible geography class I did in high school, we're talking about Denmark, Iceland, Finland, Norway, and Sweden here. But this place is not just for those with Viking blood. Its doors are open to everyone. The architecture itself is inspired by Viking ships, birch forests, and rune stones and is truly impressive. Inside, there is an exhibit hall that hosts traveling art and other cultural exhibits with Nordic themes and a great hall that hosts all kinds of events and Nordic activities. Nordia House celebrates all the Nordic holidays and offers workshops like

NORDIA HOUSE

What: Nordic cultural center

Where: 8800 SW Oleson Rd.

Cost: Free

Pro Tip: Fogelbo House is on the grounds, built by legendary Henry Steiner and registered as a National Historic Place. They offer tours once a year in May.

Nordia may be the only place in town to get a proper game of Nordic Kubb—a combination of lawn bowling and horseshoes, and sometimes called Viking Chess.

Top: *A game of Nordic Kubb*

Left: *Inset of Nordia's Leroy Setziol door*

Dala horse carving, basket weaving, and Nordic knitting circles. There's a Swedish café, Broder Söder, where you can get some delicious aebleskiver (Danish pancakes) and a gift shop where you can pick up a Nordic flag and some Finnish candy. Walking paths circle the building and are home to beautiful rain gardens. It's Portland, so bring your dog.

WORST DAY OF THE YEAR RIDE

How can you prove your devotion to cycling while perhaps dressing up as a panda?

Despite the name of this event, "Worst Day of the Year Ride" is actually the most optimistic event of the year. It is a testament to the dedication of Portland bikers. "Yeah, it's going to get drizzly and cold in late winter," this event says, "and we're going to smile and party and bike our way through it." Each year, organizers try to predict a day on the calendar that is likely to be really terrible and schedule a group ride. Because this is Portland, people started wearing goofy costumes to pedal around in, and a giant costume contest is part of the official event. Prizes are awarded in four categories: weather-themed, most elaborate, group, and punniest. Again, because this is Portland, the whole thing must start off with group coffee. Once everyone's had a chance to get caffeinated and doughnut-ed, a drum corps announces the beginning of the ride and cyclists are off

WORST DAY OF THE YEAR RIDE

What: Cycling event

Where: Check worstdayride.com for routes

Cost: $65 for adults, ages 15 and younger ride free

Pro Tip: Proceeds benefit the Community Cycling Center, which, among many other things, delivers refurbished bikes to kids from low-income backgrounds.

Despite all attempts to schedule for bad weather, Portland usually provides a lovely day for the event. Go figure.

on their choice of multiple routes. There's a half-time party in the middle and a big after-party at the end, complete with a five-story chocolate fountain that I interpret as an homage to the mud and gushing waterfalls that result from the winter rains.

THE SPORTS BRA

Where can a person go to actually watch a women's team, even if there is a men's sport happening at the same time?

Even in Portland, home of our beloved Thorns and Rose City Rollers, women's sports get less attention than men's. Women's sports have been underrepresented and have received less money since . . . well, at least since there have been televised sports. And whether you care about sports or not, what kind of message are we sending out to young girls about their worth compared to boys? It's a problem that's bigger than one city, or even one nation, so what can one little business do?

THE SPORTS BRA

What: A bar for women's sports and more

Where: 2512 NE Broadway

Cost: I get the tempeh Reuben for $14.

Pro Tip: Best-named drink is the Title IX, named after the gender equity law passed in 1972 that banned sex discrimination in federally funded education programs.

The Sports Bra hopes to be that small ripple that leads to big waves. Besides our living rooms, where do most sports get watched? Sports bars. It's a great place to start making a difference. Portland chef Jenny Nguyen was frustrated with the lack of places available to watch women's sports with her friends. They would joke about opening their own place, switching a few letters around, and calling it the Sports Bra.

Nguyen's partner convinced her to make it a reality after much talk of how she could make a positive change in the world. Ultimately, Nguyen found a place on Broadway that would do the job.

Opened in April of 2022, the Sports Bra is the first women's sports bar in the world. They feature any women's sports competitions that are available on television, cable, or satellite.

Tobin Heath of the Portland Thorns in the '16 playoffs, courtesy of Roscoe Myrick Shotboxer.com

When no game is being aired, they fill the dead air with women's podcasts, interviews, documentaries, and more. The space is decked out as you'd imagine, full of women's sports memorabilia and posters. What I hadn't imagined is that their menu would showcase women as well. Nguyen sources from as many women-owned businesses as she can. Products from local women-owned ranches and farms dominate the menu. And the drink list features Freeland Spirits, a women-owned and -operated distillery that even sources its grain from women's farms. Furniture comes from Girls Build, a nonprofit that teaches carpentry skills to girls.

Can boys go here? This boy does. Many do. The owners stress that "The Sports Bra is not a sports bar for women, but a bar for women's sports!" And since the idea is to ultimately help the next generation of women, all ages are allowed here.

To put it in perspective: "Forty percent of athletes are women," said Jenny Nguyen. "Ninety-six percent of all athletes on TV are men."

TAKE A LEFT AT THE FORK

Is it worth the forking trip?

I was finished writing this book when I picked up the paper and saw the news: "World's Biggest Fork Arrives in Fairview Today." Stop the presses, right? It's still pending Guinness certification as of this writing. But the current record belongs to a fork in Springfield, Missouri, and that little cocktail fork only measures in at 35 feet. Our fork is 37 feet long, which is two more fork-feet, so it's only a formality. It weighs 2.5 tons, they say, which makes me wonder where the world's biggest scale must be. The Fairview Fork stands, appropriately enough, at the corner of the new Fairview Food Plaza. In Portland fashion, there will be cuisine from all over the world, pop-up vendors (we loooove our food trucks around here), and, of course, a beer garden that will feature local brews.

THE WORLD'S LARGEST FORK

What: Impractically large cutlery

Where: NE Halsey St. and NE 223rd Ave.

Cost: Free, but you're going to want to spend money at one of the food trucks there.

Pro Tip: There's a large *F* stamped on the top of the fork. For Fairview? Fork? Food trucks? Nobody's saying.

Why a giant fork exactly? They left a spot for "something" decorative there, maybe a windmill or a water tower . . . they

---

The steel fork is actually 40 feet tall, but the tines pierce the ground three feet below.

weren't sure what, and one of the designers suggested they "put a fork in it," until they could decide what to put there. Referring to it as "the fork" long enough put it in their heads that an actual fork was a pretty good idea. And, of course, it will allow us all to make that "take a left at the fork in the road" joke, which I know we're all looking forward to.

THE SALMON ON SALMON ABOVE THE SALMON

Where is the most appropriately placed sculpture in the entire world?

Sculptor Keith Jellum is responsible for the extremely Portland-ish eleven-foot-long bronze salmon that can be seen thrashing its way through the bricks on the corner of one of our downtown buildings. Where? Salmon Street, of course. Where on Salmon Street? Above a restaurant that serves salmon.

It's bizarre and awesome, so it belongs in this book. But it is also hidden much of the year, depending on what the trees surrounding it are doing. You would be surprised how many people miss a giant fish crashing (or is he just happily swimming?) through the corner bricks of a building. But even when the trees are balding, the fish swims high above eye level (it's on the third floor), so you really need to be looking up.

TRANSCENDENCE

What: Giant thrashing salmon sculpture

Where: Third floor, above Southpark Seafood at NW corner of Salmon St. and SW Park Ave.

Cost: Free

Pro Tip: The piece is actually called *Transcendence*, but locals prefer *Fishzilla*.

Keith Jellum is a Portland-based artist, and he has at least two other sculptures in the city that you should visit. One can be found on Morrison Street, between 9th and 10th Avenues downtown. Again, you have to look up to see it, as it actually hovers above the sidewalk. Created in 1984, it's entitled *Electronic Poet*, or simply E. P. It's a little over four feet long, made of bronze and an LED light board that displays a curated

The salmon on Salmon above the salmon

collection of poetry that loops around like the sign on a city bus. The poems change (very roughly) every six months and are picked by Jellum himself.

The other is called *Mimir*, and it's more of what you might consider a traditional sculpture, made of bronze and placed at ground level where it's easy to see. But the sculpture itself is certainly unique. Mimir was a figure from Norse mythology known for his great wisdom. He is beheaded in battle, at which point Odin carries his head around because it still gives really great advice. You will not get that from looking at this piece. I see an alien fishlike thing with tusks and perhaps wearing shoulder pads. Jellum himself says it is "part fish, part space creature." Also, there is a plaque with nonsensical hieroglyphics. Don't try to decipher it. You will fail.

It's the most sensible thing about our city.

THE FLIGHTIEST MAUSOLEUM YOU'LL EVER SEE

What has many wings but cannot fly?

The answer is the Portland Memorial Mausoleum. Wings, you say? Yes, says I. The outside of the building is the canvas for the nation's largest hand-painted mural—one that depicts a great blue heron and many other feathered friends. The mausoleum is eight stories, and the mural covers about 43,485 square feet. You can't see it from space, but you can see it from the I-5 as well as from a lot of other places in town. Painted by Dan Cohen of ArtFX Murals and Shane Bennett, the Regional Arts and Culture Council says it "highlights the importance of the 160 acre Oaks Bottom Wildlife Refuge to the city of Portland's quality of life, the contribution of the wetland system as a critical element of the city's green infrastructure, and its contribution to maintaining biodiversity in the city and metropolitan area." All that talk of wetlands and urban biodiversity? That's all due to Mike Houck, who not only conceived of the mural but also saved that wetland.

YES, THEY PUT A BIRD ON IT

What: The country's largest hand-painted mural

Where: 6705 SE 14th Ave.

Cost: Free

Pro Tip: When you go to visit the mural up close, stop by Oaks Amusement Park, open since 1905 and one of the oldest in the country.

Mike tells the story that inspiration struck as he came across a muralist painting a beer bottle in 1991. He tracked down the company, ArtFX Murals, and asked for a volunteer to paint a

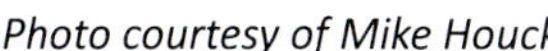
Photo courtesy of Mike Houck

great blue heron on the lower west-facing wall of the mausoleum. The owner, Mark Bennett, not loving the view of the "butt-ugly" gray mausoleum he happened to live across from, was game. The city fell in love and wanted the rest of the building done as well, but the $20,000 proved too difficult to raise. Long story short, Bennett and Houck came together 27 years later to see if they could try again. Mark and his son, Shane, were willing to do it for one-sixth the going rate, but that still left 30 grand to raise, which they ultimately did through grants and donations. The mural itself is the collaborative gumbo of Mike, Audubon Society of Portland's Bob Sallinger, local artist Dan Cohen, and Shane. The four of them refined Mark's original rough sketch, creating "a wetland motif that featured both migratory species and year-round residents of Oaks Bottom." The last addition was an Anna's hummingbird that kept buzzing Shane's face as he tried to paint.

The mural was dedicated in October of 2009, and Shane would tragically die in a snowmobile accident the following winter. The memorial service was on the roof of the mausoleum and mourners took note of the bald eagle—known to be one of Shane's favorites—that circled overhead a few times before skying out toward the Willamette River.

Besides getting the giant great blue heron painted on the wall overlooking the wetlands, Mike Houck also spearheaded the effort to make the great blue heron Portland's official city bird, which it is!

CREEPY'S

Where should I go if I'm really down to clown?

If you're looking for a drink and you really want to get your Portland on, look no farther than Creepy's, my favorite bar in east Portland. If you're looking to chase back a veggie tamale with a pickletini (Reyka vodka, Dolin dry, and MoonBrine pickle juice), this is your place.

But the real reason to come to Creepy's is the atmosphere. I'm not sure how best to describe it. Clown cozy? Carny chic? The joint is packed with vintage clown paintings, mechanical tin toys from the '50s, velvet portraits of bug-eyed children, and taxidermy.

If this were any other city, Creepy's would have been a weird-on-purpose tourist attraction, probably owned by whomever owns TGI Fridays. But this is Portland, and the atmosphere is created from the genuine love of its co-owners. They simply wanted to run a tavern where there was always something interesting to look at and proceeded to decorate it with items from their personal collections. As their curatorial tastes run right alongside mine, the name Creepy's seems apt.

CREEPY'S

What: A very creepy pub

Where: 627 SE Morrison St.

Cost: Jim's white pants (a rum concoction) is $10.

Pro Tip: Closed Mondays so the employees can clown around

The coup de grâce is the five-foot-tall portrait of John Quincy Adams hanging over the bar, scanning the premises with plastic eyes that very slowly oscillate back and forth. It gives a very *Scooby Doo* vibe to the joint.

(S)CRAP

Where can you pick up 1,000 baby jar lids, the skeleton of a piano, or a barrel of bottle caps?

Some people call it "upcycling," but at SCRAP, they inspire us to get creative rather than always utilitarian with others' discards. Every time I pop in, they've got barrels of new stuff. You will find the regular cardboard tubes, vintage magazines, stickers, buttons, popsicle sticks, and marbles; that's a given. But there is a constant influx of weirdness and rarities, which is why I return regularly: racoon tail nubs, piano hammers, robot kits, and plastic fangs. Some are great finds of single items. But the real inspiration comes with the ridiculous volume. What could you do with 10,000 film canisters? Eight million crayons? Six hundred CDs? I have to leave it for you—my wife won't let me bring anything home from SCRAP anymore until I find a use for the 90 soup spoons I picked up there earlier this year.

SCRAP began in 1998 as a place for teachers to deposit all of their leftover classroom materials. What do you do with all those extra bottles of paste you bought? Put them on a table for other teachers to use, that's what. A year and an environmental grant later, SCRAP was on its way to becoming a nonprofit holy land for Portlanders in search of cheap materials.

SCRAP VS. CRAP

What: Creative reuse center

Where: 1736 SW Alder St.

Cost: Free to enter. Two handfuls of pens is a dollar.

Pro Tip: Parking is very limited so plan accordingly.

You can throw parties here too (kids or adults), with a host to lead you through an art project with all the fixin's.

BABY GOAT THERAPY

What can you do about all that stress?

I've mentioned elsewhere in this book about the labyrinths Portland has to offer. And we've no lack of places to forest bathe or sit and stare at the mountains. But sometimes you need the big guns. Sometimes you need a baby Nigerian dwarf goat to take a nap in your arms. That's a thing? YES! THAT'S A THING! For a measly 10 bucks an hour (per person), you can cuddle a baby goat. You know what else you can do? Baby goat yoga. Or maybe you want some Nigerian dwarf goats at your wedding or your office party, so that you have something to counteract the stress from looking at your boss's face. Portland Goat Parties is here to save us all. They're a small, family-owned operation, and this is no petting zoo. These goats are their family goats, super loved and cared for. They bought a property in 2017 that was overrun with blackberries, and a Portlander will tell you that what you need to cure a blackberry problem is a goat. So they goated up, starting with Chloe, Lucy, and Steve. Five seasons later, enough kids have been born on the farm to take care of business.

PORTLAND GOAT PARTIES

What: Baby Nigerian dwarf goats!

Where: 19457 SW McCormick Hill Rd.

Cost: You can hold a goat for just $10 an hour.

Pro Tip: If you want that goat cuddle, you'll be going out to the farm and you'll want to schedule that with portlandgoatparties.com.

When those goats are not clearing brush, they're ready to take a nap with you, do some yoga, or just party.

THE KENNEDY SCHOOL

Where can you relive high school detention, but this time with a drink in your hand and a basket of tater tots?

There is something very creepy about wandering alone in the halls of a dimly lit, century-old school at night. When I first visited, I couldn't determine whether all of these old photos on the walls and downright eerie painting of children were supposed to be frightening or if it just happened that way—like clowns and children singing nursery rhymes. I still don't know. What I know is this: The school was built in 1915 and was abandoned by the time McMenamins (a Portland-based pub and hotel juggernaut) bought and renovated it in the '90s. They turned 57 classrooms into guest rooms, keeping everything as close to its roots as possible, right down to the original chalkboards on the walls. The old cafeteria is now a courtyard restaurant. You can watch a movie in the old auditorium. Various other rooms contain a gift shop, brewery, and soaking pool.

THE KENNEDY SCHOOL

What: A historic high-school-turned-hotel, bar, theater, and brewery. Also? Haunted.

Where: 5736 NE 33rd Ave.

Cost: Free to roam and look around

Pro Tip: Once a girls' restroom, Concordia Brewery now brews local favorites here like Whiskey Widow and Yule Shoot Your Eye Out! Double IPA.

My favorite features are the various small bars, including the Detention Bar, where you can get fine whiskey and cigars, just like at my old high school.

SOURCES

Mondo Croquet
https://mondocroquet.com

Well, I'll Be Horse-Tied
Site visits, https://www.atlasobscura.com/places/portland-horse-rings

Hippo Hardware
Site visit. Interview with employees.

Lost Nihonmachi (Japantown)
https://www.streetroots.org/news/2019/01/11/when-portland-had-largest-japantown-oregon

Zelda the Bulldog
Site visit. https://www.dogster.com/lifestyle/zelda-english-bulldog-carol-gardner-interview

The Chapman Swifts
Site visit. Interview with Audubon Society guides.

Una, the Professional Mermaid
https://www.unathemermaid.com

Ota Tofu
https://www.otapdx.com/our-story

Madness!
Site visit. https://moviemadness.org

Yoda's House
Site visit. https://www.oregonlive.com/life-and-culture/g66l-2019/06/b8c9e072e54963/what-happened-to-the-wacky-9dome-west-linn-hobbit-house-see-for-yourself-.html

The Zymoglyphic Museum
Site visit. Interview with Jim Stewart.

Resistance Is Futel
http://futel.net

The Friendliest Sculpture in Town
Interview with Pete Beeman: https://trimet.org/publicart/greenline.htm

Dinosaur Flies
https://ucanr.edu/blogs/blogcore/postdetail.cfm?postnum=24815

Zoobomb Pyle
Site visit. https://bikeportland.org/cats/the-scene/zoobomb

Monkey Puzzle Trees
https://www.oregonlive.com/opinion/2011/07/save_the_monkey_puzzle_tree.html

Sauvie Island UFO
Site visit. The blog of Erik Gauger: https://www.notesfromtheroad.com

Puirks—Portland Quirks Part 1
Personal observations and anonymous interviews.

The World's Largest Lawn Zoo
Site visit. https://www.mikebennettart.com

York: Terra Incognita
Site visit. https://www.lclark.edu/visit/features/york

Yes Surrey
Interview with Kerr Bikes. https://www.albertinakerr.org/support-our-work/kerr-bikes

Twin Pines Country Club
Site visit. http://twinpinescountryclub.com

Love Lock Bridge
Site Visit.

Puirks—Part 2
Personal observations and anonymous interviews.

Mad Doc Raven's Place
Site visit. https://www.ravensmanorexperience.com

The Portland Troll Bridge
Site visit.

The Second-Oldest Tiki Bar in the Country
Site visit. https://www.bucketlistbars.com/travelogues/146-the-second-oldest-tiki-bar-in-the-country-the-alibi-tiki-lounge

Slap Taggin'
Site visits. Chats with local artists.

Jan Brady Waterfall
Site visit. Personal observation.

The Great Willamette Boat of Ill Repute
http://www.offbeatoregon.com/H1007d_floating-bordello-in-portland.html, Holbrook, Stewart. Wildmen, Wobblies and Whistle Punks. Corvallis: OSU Press

Most Gorge-ous View (Sorry, Not Sorry)
Site visit and personal observation.

Stark Naked on Stark Street
https://www.oregonlive.com

Paths to Inner Peace
https://labyrinthlocator.com

Bike Lane Art Installations
BikePortland (https://bikeportland.org)

A Museum That Really Sucks
https://starks.com

The Portland Pickles
https://www.portlandpicklesbaseball.com

Ghosts and Garlic Knots
https://theghostinmymachine.com

The Free Pittock View and Orientation
Site visit and personal observation.

Dr. Tongue's I Had That Shoppe
Site visit and personal observation.

Puirks—Part 3
Site visit and personal observation.

The Witch House
Site visit.

Darcelle XV
https://www.darcellexv.com/

***She Who Watches* (*Tsagaglalal*)**
https://www.oregonhikers.org/field_guide/She_Who_Watches_Hike, https://www.archaeology.org/issues/257-1705/from-the-trenches/5453-trenches-washington-columbia-hills

***Jerry*, Patron Saint of South Waterfront**
Site visit. walkingpdx.com, https://www.thenatureofcities.com/2019/02/10/beaver-cottonwoods-lucy-preservation-not-enough

Three Groins in a Fountain
Site visit. https://en.wikipedia.org/wiki/The_Quest_(Portland,_Oregon)

Velkristan's Nirvana
Site visit. https://kcymaerxthaere.com

A Game of Brutal Beauty
https://www.rosecityrollers.com

Woody Woodpecker's Laugh
http://www.pdxhistory.com/html/mel_blanc.html,https://orjewishlife.com/portlands-mel-blanc

***Twilight* Swan House**
https://www.weirdhomestour.com/homes/twilight

The Golden West Hotel
https://www.blackpast.org/african-american-history/golden-west-hotel-portland-1906-1931/, https://www.oregonencyclopedia.org/articles/golden_west_hotel/#.YkIVDLhlCAo

The Most Loved Carpet in the World
Site Visit. https://www.pdxmonthly.com/news-and-city-life/2019/09/a-brief-history-of-that-whole-pdx-airport-carpet-thing

Spud Puppy Passion
Site visits. Observations. https://www.oregonlive.com/business/2014/11/tater_tots_a_snack_with_oregon.html

Rimsky-Korsakoffee House
Site visit. Interview with employees and customers.

Crimping in Stumptown
https://www.oregonencyclopedia.org/articles/shanghai_tunnels_myth/#.YkIVqbhlCAo, https://pdxsocialhistory.org/stories/crimping.html

A Great Time with Some Strings Attached
Site visit. http://www.puppetmuseum.com

Royal Rosarians Milk Carton Races
https://eastpdxnews.com/general-news-features/class-teaches-how-make-a-milk-carton-boat-that-floats-2

The Freakybuttrue Peculiarium
Site visit. Interview with employees.

Lincoln Street Kayak and Canoe Museum
https://www.atlasobscura.com/places/lincoln-street-kayak-and-canoe-museum

Benson Bubblers
portlandoregon.gov

Adult Soap Box Derby
Interview with Jason de Parrie-Turner, https://www.soapboxracer.com

A Five-Volcano Day
Personal interviews with Oregonians.

***The Simpsons* Tour**
Site visits. https://www.travelportland.com/culture/simpsons-landmarks

Remembering Vanport
vanportmosaic.org, https://www.streetroots.org/news/2018/04/20/life-and-death-vanport-70-years-after-flood

The Captain's Wheel at Dan and Louis Oyster Bar
Site Visit. http://www.offbeatoregon.com/o1101b-shipwreck-of-brother-jonathan-ground-zero-in-fight-over-treasure.html

Portland Street Art Alliance
Interview with Portland Street Art Alliance, pdxstreetart.org

The Portland Podiums
Site visit. https://trimet.org/publicart

Squatchin' It Up
northamericanbigfootcenter.com

Paul Boneyan vs. Paul Bunyan
Site visits.

And Speaking of Skeletons
Site visit and personal observation.

Signs of the Times
Site visit. Interview with Kate Widdows.

Hidden Tea Wizards
Site visit. http://flyawakepdx.com/

Underground Drinking
Site visit and personal observation.

The Mysterious Portland Weather Machine
Site visit, https://www.oregonlive.com/portland/2020/01/portlands-whimsical-weather-machine-has-been-forecasting-from-pioneer-courthouse-square-since-1988.html

World's Tallest Barber Pole
Site visit, https://www.oregonlive.com/forest-grove/2013/03/worlds_tallest_barber_pole_was.html

Setziol Doors
https://www.modernhomesportland.com/leroy-setziol-pacific-northwest-sculptor/, https://atticgallery.com/product-category/leroy-setziol

The Other Independent Bookstores
Site visit and personal observation.

Nursery Rhyme Nightmare Juice
Site visit. https://www.enchantedforest.com

A Contest for the Chickenhearted
http://www.lentschickencontest.com/

Dragon Boats
https://www.portlanddragonboats.com/, https://rootsrated.com/stories/why-you-should-try-dragon-boat-paddling-in-portland-this-spring

Nordia House
Site visit. https://www.nordicnorthwest.org

Worst Day of the Year Ride
https://worstdayride.com

The Sports Bra
thesportsbrapdx.com, https://pdx.eater.com/2022/2/18/22941255/the-sports-bra-bar-wnba-nwsl

Take a Left at the Fork
https://www.worldrecordacademy.org/world-records/world-s-largest-fork-fairview-s-giant-fork-sets-world-record 422150

The Flightiest Mausoleum You'll Ever See
Interviews with Mike Houck

Creepy's
Site visit, lots of drinks and chats with bartenders.

(S)Crap
Site visit. https://portland.scrapcreativereuse.org/SCRAP-History

Baby Goat Therapy
https://www.portlandgoatparties.com/

The Kennedy School
Site visit.

INDEX